WORKFORCE INTELLIGENCE

Mike Sullivan | Vinay Gidwaney

WORKFORCE INTELLIGENCE

The **PEOPLE-FIRST** Playbook for Leading Your Company Through **AI TRANSFORMATION**

WILEY

Published by John Wiley & Sons, Inc., Hoboken, New Jersey.

For general information on our other products and services or for technical support, please contact our Customer Care Department within the United States at (800) 762-2974, outside the United States at (317) 572-3993 or fax (317) 572-4002.

Wiley also publishes its books in a variety of electronic formats. Some content that appears in print may not be available in electronic formats. For more information about Wiley products, visit our web site at www.wiley.com.

Library of Congress Cataloging-in-Publication Data is Available:

ISBN 9781394467235 (Cloth)
ISBN 9781394467242 (ePub)
ISBN 9781394467259 (ePDF)

Cover Design: Wiley
Cover Image: mitay20/Getty Images
Author Photos: Courtesy of the Authors

Printed and bound by CPI Group (UK) Ltd, Croydon, CR0 4YY

C9781394467235_060726

Contents

Foreword by Adam Bruckman *ix*

Introduction *xi*

Chapter 1 The Radiating Red Dot 1

The Book That Reshaped My Thinking 9

The Fear Factor 12

A New Framework for a New Era 14

Chapter 2 Managing Your Entire Workforce 17

Keith and the Story of Workforce Management 20

Meagan and Elizabeth: Tangible Metrics and What Comes Monday 26

Chapter 3	The Workforce Intelligence Score	31
	The Signal Is Behavioral	34
	The J-Curve	39
	Reading the Score in Four Bands	40
Chapter 4	The First Paradigm Shift: Transactional to Collaborative	43
Chapter 5	The Second Paradigm Shift: Individual to Enterprise AI Collaboration	59
Chapter 6	Start with the Job Description	71
	Where to Start	76
	Writing the Job Description	82
	Specialist Coworkers	86
Chapter 7	Hiring Ben: The Three-Phase Lifecycle	91
	Phase One: Internship	94
	Phase Two: Apprenticeship	96
	Phase Three: Full-Time	99
	Ongoing Supervisor Education	101
Chapter 8	Building the Hybrid Workforce	105
	The Five-Tier Fluency Model	112
	Three Types of AI in the Hybrid Workforce	119
	Training as a Sustained Cadence	124
Chapter 9	The Paradox of AI in Our Image	129
	Why They Have Faces	132

	The Work-Life and Personal-Life Line	136
	The Reframe Stories	138
	Addressing Assumptions About AI	143
Chapter 10	Owning Your Intelligence	149
	Build on Top of the Models	154
	Make the Intelligence Visible	156
	Build the Intelligence Map	157
	Compounding Intelligence	161
Chapter 11	The Humanity Test	165
	The Faces	167
	The Humanity Test	168
	A Word We Use Every Day Now	170
	What Only the Blended Workforce Can Build	171
	The Deal That Has to Be Made	172
	The Partnership That Wrote This Book	174
	What We Still Do Not Know	175
	A Final Word	175

Appendices 177

Appendix A: The WI Score Calculator 179

Appendix B: For the Individual Employee: Your Personal WI Playbook 183

Appendix C: The Work Center Framework and Irreducibility Test 187

Appendix D: The Coworker Job Description Template and Opportunity Scorecard 195

Appendix E: The Hybrid Workforce Architecture 199

Appendix F: The Intelligence Map Starter Guide 201

Appendix G: Monday Morning Checklist 203

Notes 207

Acknowledgments 215

About the Authors 217

Index 219

Foreword

THERE ARE MOMENTS in the life of a company that you recognize as defining, even as you are living them. The work you hold in your hands came out of one of those moments.

Mike Sullivan and I have been building OneDigital together for decades. Through every defining moment, we have approached change with fresh thinking and a forward-looking mindset. This book is an expression of that same spirit.

Five years ago, we added a critical voice to that partnership. Vinay Gidwaney is one of the most gifted technologists and sharpest minds I have encountered in my career. What has made his partnership even more valuable to our team and to this organization goes well beyond his technical expertise. Vinay's greatest gift is his clarity about what actually drives successful transformation: not the technology itself, but how people evolve alongside it and how an organization manages change. That insight has cascaded across OneDigital in ways that are difficult to overstate and, in many ways, is one of the core foundations of this work.

This book and the Workforce Intelligence framework are the product of Mike and Vinay's partnership and their unwavering passion to drive our organization forward. The transformation we now find ourselves in is the most significant to date and the firms that treat it as a technology upgrade will miss what is really at stake. Mike and Vinay understood this early and acted. They did not wait for the playbook to exist. *Workforce Intelligence* is the framework that emerged from their work.

My confidence in the path ahead is not just rooted in our decades of evolution and executing when the stakes are highest. It is also rooted in the passion, curiosity, and trust of our 6,000 team members that have always been at the core of this organization. I am enormously proud of what we are building and thrilled that Mike and Vinay chose to share it so our clients and other organizations can benefit from our real-time learnings.

When you read this book, you will encounter a framework that applies to every organization navigating today's AI uncertainty. You will also encounter a pair of entrepreneurs who are completely honest about their explorations, their confidence and excitement for the future, and their fear of the unknown. That honesty is one of the things I admire most about this work.

—Adam Bruckman
Co-founder and CEO, OneDigital
Atlanta, Georgia

Introduction

I HAVE A confession to make.

Some mornings, I wake up, and the possibilities seem endless. AI is going to change what we at OneDigital can do for clients in ways I am only beginning to understand, and the urgency I feel has no precedent in the prior decades of helping to build this company.

Other mornings, I wake up very early and sit with the house quiet around me, running the same questions on a loop and arriving, each time, at the same unsettling conclusion.

AI scares me.

Perhaps it scares you, too.

What I have come to understand is that both of those mornings are telling me the truth. The possibilities are real. So is the fear.

I have felt this kind of fear before. That is important, and I will come back to it. But the only honest place to start a book like this one is in the space between those feelings.

My name is Mike Sullivan. I am a history major with no coding background. I co-founded OneDigital, an insurance advisory and financial services firm with 6,000 colleagues, 100,000 employer clients, and over 10 million American and Canadian families that depend on the quality of our firm's advice. Over the last 26 years, I have needed to make business decisions in moments of uncertainty more often than I can count. I have been wrong in expensive ways and right in inexplicable ways. Thanks to this experience, I can recognize the signs of an industry in transition. . . An industry that needs to get moving.

My co-author, Vinay Gidwaney, is a serial entrepreneur who never finished university and who has spent three decades building software companies. During the pandemic, he helped run the mass vaccination sites at Fenway Park and Gillette Stadium, which were moving 10,000 people a day. He joined OneDigital in 2021 because his wife made him promise to trade startups for something more established. What he has brought to our company is a systems-thinking approach forged in the fires of multiple successful startups.

Vinay and I view our partnership as that of two operators. The thinking in these pages was built inside a live business, under real pressure, in real time, through the discomfort of being right, then wrong, adjusting, and trying again.

I have worked with hundreds of talented people at OneDigital. The partnership I have with Vinay is different in a way I find difficult to put into words. He is a senior leader and an intellectual peer, and his professional life has run on a clock I still don't understand. His instincts were formed in environments where you shipped code at midnight, ran out of payroll twice in the same year, pivoted a product over a weekend because you had no choice, and measured success in software releases rather than client relationships. Our nervous systems are wired differently, and that difference produces a kind of thinking neither of us could reach alone. And honestly, it's the kind of collaborative thinking I believe every company needs to use when dealing with artificial intelligence.

What I want you to understand, before anything else, is that the fear I described in the opening paragraph is not a weakness in this story. It is the engine driving it forward. When Vinay and I faced the sudden inevitability of a dramatic AI transformation, we drew on over 50 years of combined experience dealing with similar challenges. This wasn't the first time change had threatened a company under our leadership. Our past has taught us how to channel our fears into meaningful forward movement.

In April of 2000, my wife, Patti, and I sat at our kitchen table in the early wreckage of the dot-com collapse. At the time, OneDigital was one of many dot-com companies in trouble. I told Patti that I might need to find a new job. Thanks to some creative thinking and a little bit of luck, we were able to see OneDigital through that early near-death experience.

In 2010, the Affordable Care Act rewrote the ground rules of the small-employer benefits business. The model that had carried us out of the first crisis was suddenly operating under regulatory conditions it was not designed for. Our team had to move quickly to evolve our business model for the new environment under the ACA.

Then, in the spring of 2020, a global pandemic hit the whole world at once, and a firm built entirely on in-person advisory relationships had to figure out how to maintain and strengthen those relationships through laptop screens.

Each of those moments felt unsurvivable in the days before the path forward appeared. And each time, what got us through was not a plan we had made in advance. It was the willingness to move incrementally forward with the facts we had and a directional north star, combined with enough accumulated trust inside our organization to make the action credible.

The emergence of AI is the fourth time I've felt like OneDigital is facing unprecedented, company-threatening change. However, this time my fears differ slightly from those in the first three instances. The dot-com collapse was a business-model problem that took over two and a half years to resolve once we built something the market was willing to fund. The

ACA was a regulatory problem with discoverable contours, and once we mapped the contours, we could build inside them. Even the pandemic, for all its severity, arrived with a visible end somewhere on the horizon. AI has no horizon. It's here to stay.

AI is going to produce remarkable advances across many fields of human endeavor, including medicine, engineering, scientific research, education, and the creative arts. In most of those fields, the changes will be essentially linear. There will be faster diagnoses, better modeling, richer creative tools, and improvements that arrive on a curve that existing frameworks can accommodate. Many of these types of organizations can adapt in a reasonably orderly way.

Conversely, AI's effect on knowledge-based organizations will not be linear. The technology itself makes information accessible at a commercial scale. It also enables analysis, ideation, and relatively informed decision-making for individual contributors. As a result, if knowledge-based organizations do not evolve their business models, their economics will come under material pressure.

The window to adapt is now, and the time to react is shortening.

Every prior significant challenge in our company's history has followed the same arc. Once we realized what was at stake, the fear drove us to meaningful action. We reinvented our company and evolved our business to provide value that exceeded our expectations. After the dot-com collapse, we produced a $45 million outsourcing business that had never been seen in our industry. The ACA reinvention required us to pivot from managing accounts for the largest brokers in the country to acquiring retail benefits firms directly, a model nobody had operated at OneDigital's scale. By the time the pandemic was over, our client service cadence was so effective that clients still reference it years later as the moment they knew they had the right partner.

AI has introduced the same arc, except the territory on the other side of our fears is categorically larger than the territory we crossed in any of the prior three crises. Today, we are delivering services to our clients that were not available twelve months ago, and the list of new capabilities is expanding faster than we can fully absorb. We can deliver in-the-moment insights at a depth that used to require weeks of analyst work. We can run analyses simultaneously across thousands of employer relationships in less time than a single review used to take. Complex actuarial and regulatory questions, the ones that used to leave a CFO confused or a benefits manager anxious, now resolve into clear answers in real time.

The fear of being displaced drove us to work in ways more client-centric than many of us believed possible. Where our AI transformation will land us is still uncertain. Most of the path forward remains unstructured. The direction, however, is undoubtedly forward. And the possibilities are extraordinary.

AI is, fundamentally, a people challenge that technology has made unavoidable. The organizations navigating the transition most effectively have technology leaders and people leaders sitting in the same room, thinking through problems together, and arriving at solutions neither group could have reached alone. Vinay and I do that every day, and the framework we have built is a direct product of that practice.

Many organizations will need to build their own version of this partnership at the leadership level. They will need to actively combine technology thinking and people thinking together in the rooms where leaders make consequential decisions. That combination is frighteningly (and unnecessarily) rare and yet has never been more essential.

A major reason for writing this book is our core belief that every firm will face a defining choice. AI will, at some point, force leaders to choose directly between people and profit: between reinvesting the capacity AI returns into the people who built the business and pocketing it as profit margin. That decision, and what it reveals about a firm's character, is what we call the humanity test. It is the question this entire book is preparing you to answer, and we save our full reckoning with it for the final pages. As for OneDigital, I can tell you unequivocally that my co-founding partner, Adam Bruckman, and I did not spend the last 26 years building this company for the long term only to have AI render its people obsolete. Our decision is made. The harder work is helping you arrive at yours.

Theory plays a minuscule role in this book. The methodology Vinay and I present was built within a complex advisory business with an award-winning culture. We figured out this playbook in real time alongside thousands of colleagues who were counting on us to get it right.

The future we are building toward is bright and, admittedly, still a little bit uncertain. Capabilities that do not yet exist will exist within a year and reshape our thinking again. Client conversations we have not yet had will open possibilities we cannot currently picture. None of that uncertainty diminishes the clarity of the direction.

What follows is a real playbook, built and stress-tested inside an operating company. Read it for the methodology. But know that the methodology is in service of a choice waiting for you at the end, and that choice is the reason any of this matters.

The direction is forward. The pace must be fast. Let's begin.

1

The Radiating Red Dot

The screen was the only light in the room, and had been for hours.

It was sometime past five in the morning, and I sat at my desk running on coffee and a feeling close to wonder, laced with dread.

Six weeks earlier, Vinay had helped me set up Claude AI and a software platform called Replit. He did so mostly to satisfy a fixation he described, generously, as my "dopamine fix." He was also helping me address a question that had been bothering me for weeks.

What would AI disruption do to our business, our industry, and the premise on which we had built a company with $1.5 billion in revenue?

On an otherwise unremarkable evening that started around eight o'clock, I was doing what no reasonable person who knew me would have predicted. Having never touched a line of code in my life, I was building a software program.

I am OneDigital's co-founder, our growth guy, our storyteller, and our value-proposition architect, a guy always looking toward the horizon, trying to understand the road ahead. I am about as far away from a software programmer as a person can get.

A year earlier, the people who knew me would have laughed at the idea of Mike Sullivan spending a night writing code. The laughter would have been audible from the parking lot. I mean, I majored in history! Yet there I was, pulling the programmer's trademark all-nighter, iterating on software puzzles to design an app that would solve my most pressing concern.

Around six in the morning, I succeeded. The image on my screen was extraordinary.

With no coding experience, I built a working software tool in ten hours. In a single overnight, I accomplished what would traditionally have required weeks of professional developer time, a scoping process, a roadmap, and a budget in the tens of thousands of dollars. How was this possible?

My experience went well beyond the convenience of a super-powerful new technological gadget. My all-nighter was a *partnership* with a form of intelligence, and that collaboration expanded the boundaries of my own capabilities. I wanted to think more about that, except I couldn't focus on that insight at the moment because a different realization was causing my heart rate to increase.

On my screen, in the app I had developed, was a radiating red dot. That dot confirmed both my greatest excitement and my worst fear.

The idea for my app was to pull together the best available research on AI disruption from leading institutions and synthesize it into a consensus view. I wanted to know where a company like OneDigital would fall on the readiness scale and to see it mapped visually. With Claude and Replit set up on my laptop, I wrote my prompts. I described what I wanted, provided all the context and information I had at my disposal, gave feedback on the program's design, and iterated until we had a product that could answer my question.

The process was addictive, and I quickly lost track of time. It was my first truly integrated AI Coworker exploration in which the final blended work product mattered at a strategic level. Around five in the morning, I wondered, *Is this what the future of work is going to feel like?*

The app pulled from fourteen sources, including McKinsey, Bain, and the World Economic Forum. These were firms that had published their own analyses of how AI would reshape industries and realign white-collar job categories. When I was sure it had all the right information and the right context for analyzing it, I gave it this prompt: "I want a four-quadrant framework that visually shows where OneDigital sits on the AI readiness scale. I want to see a dot showing exactly where we are."

More iterations followed. Then, in the early morning hours, the visual materialized.

My first reaction was amazement. The tool had done precisely what I asked, drawing from sources I could never have synthesized on my own. Not in ten hours, not in a hundred. Between dinner and sunrise, I had built my own AI-readiness assessment tool. I was quite proud of my work.

My second reaction was real concern. And I mean *real* concern.

The graph placed OneDigital in the upper-right quadrant, with a radiating red dot signaling our bad position. The diagnosis read:

> **"Without adaptation, OneDigital is susceptible to disruption from AI. You are in the asymmetry-of-information, advice-giving business, and you need to evolve what you do and how you do it."**

The consensus was that if an organization in our position did no reskilling and made no investment in augmentation, roughly a quarter of its workforce would be performing tasks that AI could do faster and at lower cost. That was the do-nothing scenario.

Vinay and I recognize that headcount reductions and margin expansion can be constructive for a company's bottom line. We are also human beings who work with other human beings, and we all need jobs to provide for our families. I felt sick at the thought that a quarter of OneDigital was doing work that could be replaced by AI.

The red dot stopped being abstract pretty quickly, replaced in my mind by the faces of people I knew.

I thought first of a benefits consultant in Maryland, a woman who had spent five years building her career by staying on calls until 9 p.m., helping a confused employee untangle a denied health insurance claim. I happen to be close friends with her parents. The data pulls and plan comparisons that filled her calendar could now be completed in seconds by AI tools. I settled my nerves with the reminder that the advisor she was on her way to becoming, the one a client would call first, was still possible. To get there, she would need to spend more of her time on the work only she could do, while the routine work that had previously consumed large parts of her workday faded into the background.

A retirement advisor in Kansas City came to mind next. Fifteen years sitting with small business owners and helping them think through what an exit might mean. He had held clients steady during 2008 when their first instinct was to sell at the bottom, and the trust he built earned him countless business referrals. However, half of his regular work week was spent on plan comparisons and contribution math, work that AI could do far faster and more accurately. I reflected on his need to rebuild his practice around the work only he could do, before AI tools that any client could open on a phone took over the rest.

I then thought about a wealth advisor in New Jersey, thirty years in, and the kind of advisor whose clients told him secrets they had not even shared with their spouses. I had to ask myself, honestly, whether the judgment he had developed over those three decades was still worth what we were charging for it. I knew he brought value to clients in ways that don't begin to fit on a spreadsheet. The question that remained was how to push this value even further and build upon what he is doing now. Otherwise, some clients might consult with AI on their own time, in an attempt to figure out how to work their finances.

Since that moment of facing the red dot, Vinay and I have come to believe that the danger to OneDigital and the people we serve lies in our own inaction. AI is not the real threat. It does not care if OneDigital survives, thrives, or dies. Inaction is the threat to our future viability.

According to my app's consensus, a quarter of our employees were performing roles whose informational and analytical components—the core tasks that filled their days—could be handled by AI at a fraction of the cost. This data does not make those people expendable. Instead, it means that without a deliberate strategy for functional expansion and role redefinition, the gap between AI capabilities and employee output would widen until the economics became impossible to ignore.

In fact, upon further investigation, the employees most exposed in the do-nothing scenario were also the ones best positioned to become the most evolved advisors the firm had ever put before clients.

The red dot demanded action.

So, what were we going to do?

Here is what we figured.

Millions of families rely on OneDigital's work. If the readiness model warned of such a fate for us, then it also held for most of our clients in some form. The HR director, trying to keep an anxious workforce informed, and the business owner, asking what AI meant for the next five years of their company, needed a guide. So did the salesperson, trying to figure out what would differentiate them in a market where the analytical layer of expertise was suddenly abundant. The same questions keeping me up at night would keep them up at night.

What if OneDigital had the solutions that could help our clients rest easy?

We could not credibly advise our clients on a transformation we had not undertaken ourselves. The firms that try to consult on AI from the outside, having read the McKinsey reports and the Boston Consulting Group (BCG) case studies without moving their own people through the change, struggle to resonate with change leaders. For OneDigital, the right path meant putting our own organization through the work first. We needed to embrace all the missteps and uncomfortable conversations that are sure to come with transforming a 6,000-plus-person organization.

We had to earn the lessons we would carry into client conversations the same way we had earned our stripes during the pandemic: by doing the work alongside our people, even as the outcome remained uncertain. A firm that undertook this evolution from within would be the one our clients would rely on in the future.

After my all-nighter, sleep was out of reach. I felt like a proud papa waiting for a recital, except my kid was a software tool that had just told me what I needed to know. I waited, anxiously, for Vinay to log on.

Vinay Gidwaney is my partner in what I sometimes call, to his ongoing horror, the story of an Irishman and an Indian who walked into a bar. He is wired for founder mode the same way some people are wired for endurance running. Vinay operates with systems thinking and an 807-slide PowerPoint deck (as of now) that contains the key ideas he has had throughout his OneDigital career. The deck, he admits, nearly crashes PowerPoint every time he opens it.

Vinay and I held a shared conviction. The companies that would survive the advent of AI were those willing to run toward the unknown. We had been playing offense for our entire careers. We had done that during the dot-com collapse, the introduction of the Affordable Care Act, and the COVID-19 pandemic. Those earlier crises had been business-model problems. The AI question threatened the value of each knowledge worker in our firm, which made the problem bigger and more urgent.

When Vinay appeared on screen that morning, I skipped the pleasantries. "*Did you see my tool?*"

He had, and he responded with a line my mind still plays on repeat. "*I love the tool. I hate what it's telling us.*"

We talked about overreaction, about whether the models were exaggerating, about all the reasons a reasonable person might dismiss the consensus and go back to running the business the way we always had. Then we stopped making excuses because neither of us believed them.

A large portion of our business today is predicated on employment. Our employer clients rely on us to help them manage their workforce, navigate benefits, manage risk, prepare for retirement, and deliver expert guidance. We exist in part because of information asymmetry, the gap between what a specialist knows and what a generalist can figure out on their own. Now we had to ask what happens when that asymmetry narrows, when the informational advantage that justifies our current fees erodes, and when the premise of our business meets a technology that makes the analytical component of our expertise abundant and accessible at low cost.

The answer, we would come to realize, depended on whether we chose to augment our people or leave them behind. That fork is not unique to OneDigital. Every firm with knowledge workers will reach the same one, and what a firm decides in that moment will say more about it than any mission statement ever could. I said to Vinay, "This is really troubling, and it's also the biggest opportunity I've ever seen."

He agreed.

The Book That Reshaped My Thinking

Months before my all-night programming session, I read a perspective-shifting book, *Co-Intelligence: Living and Working with AI*, by Ethan Mollick. Mollick is a professor at the Wharton School of the University of Pennsylvania. Vinay recommended the book to me because it had been making the rounds among AI thought leaders.[1]

I finished the book in a matter of hours.

The book opened my mind to the possibilities unlocked by the eventual partnership of AI and human users. Mollick's argument was measured and evidence-based, with implications that stunned me. His research suggested white-collar jobs in the services industry could see productivity gains of 20 to 80 percent through AI augmentation.[2]

At face value, the research sounded great. Get the right AI tools into our people's hands, and productivity would skyrocket. Yet the more I contemplated Mollick's studies and arguments, the more I realized I was thinking about AI transformation all wrong.

If I treated AI like any other technology tool, like an efficiency play, I would blunder this once-in-a-generation opportunity. The way I was thinking matched how every other executive in my network was thinking. We at OneDigital could improve baseline productivity by adopting the new technology, encouraging people to use it, measuring improvements, parting ways with those who weren't getting on board, and watching profit margins improve.

Taking such a traditional approach to AI transformation would be a career-defining mistake. The methodology might have sounded attractive on a quarterly earnings call, but it would not differentiate us or ensure our competitiveness five years down the road. If I had learned anything from Mollick's book, it was that AI transformation was the *worst* possible time to lose human workers. Why?

Artificial intelligence, however powerful, is finite. It is just a statistical model trained on a dataset. AI produces remarkable work, with bounds. Human intelligence operates by different rules.

People do not max out the way a model does, and they do not need a training set to make a connection no one has ever made before. A person carries judgment and conscience, formed by experiences no algorithm can access. Put the two intelligences together, and you get work neither would have produced in solitude.

So, the natural question is, how do we deploy human intelligence and human-AI relationships most effectively? We believe that at the enterprise level, the strength of that deployment will have an exponentially increased impact for each human partnered with our firm's AI. So, while AI will be accessible to all organizations, human intelligence for human-AI partnerships will remain scarce.

This is why AI transformation is the worst time to lose human workers.

The information advantage our industry had run on was now under pressure. AI was eating the analytical part of that advantage. The durable part of the work still took place in person, with an advisor attending to fears and interpreting data in light of each client's specific circumstances. The advisor's job is to ask the right questions and help the client arrive at a decision they can live with. Moving our people from "I know the answer" to "I know what the answer means for you" would be a demanding transition.

I called Adam Bruckman, OneDigital's CEO and my co-founder, and began cascading the message through the organization's leadership. AI offered an opportunity to reshape our value proposition in the marketplace, far beyond an efficiency play. Former limits to our capability, based solely on human capital, had vanished. New opportunities to serve our clients were ahead, limited only by our willingness to collaborate with this new intelligence.

AI is unlike every enterprise technology adopted in the last 30 years. The technology produces work that looks like it came from a thoughtful colleague. It reasons. If you ask a follow-up question, AI remembers the context, adjusts, and offers fresh analysis.

Software does not behave that way. Person-to-person behavior is closer to the experience of working with AI. This is why effective change management during AI transformation won't be led by a technology team, but by people leaders.

Here is how a typical large company introduces a new piece of enterprise software. First, the CIO is the designated leader. Then the work runs through a vendor review, a security review, a procurement cycle, an architecture map, a license agreement, and a training module that teaches employees what the new tool does and how to log in. The operations department announces the launch via a company-wide email and establishes dashboard systems to track usage and review quarterly key performance indicators. At the next review meeting, they present the utilization numbers along with a plan to improve them.

This sequence works for enterprise software deployments. For software, training is operational, and ROI is a question of the tool's efficiency. A CRM stores customer data, while an ERP processes transactions, and a project management platform organizes tasks. The IT department ensures those tools are reliable, well-integrated with the rest of the stack, and have security baked in.

AI transformation does not cleanly fit into the standard change management parameters. How do you train coworkers to develop a working relationship with a digital colleague that, upon onboarding, probably has more company knowledge than you do? Real partnerships between your people and the AI counterparts assigned to them become the metric that matters.

Run the standard IT playbook on AI, and the adoption rate lands somewhere between 15 and 20 percent, most of it concentrated among people who would have found the tools on their own.

AI transformation is fundamentally a talent management problem. Treat the work as a technology deployment, and every dollar you spend on AI will return a fraction of its potential value.

The Fear Factor

As I started making calls, I didn't reach out to the consultants, advisors, analysts, and account managers closest to clients. By that point, the frontline people had been pulling us forward, already using AI in their work and asking for more from our AI Coworker program (more on this later). They had quietly demonstrated what was possible. For over two years, they had been ahead of the average leader in our industry.

My calls went to fellow leaders, the people running practices, regions, business lines, and senior functions. Their decisions would either accelerate the AI transformation or leave it on hold for another quarter. Those leaders needed the activation moment I experienced after my all-nighter. They needed to feel, in their gut as much as their head, that the trajectory of their work was about to shift, irrespective of their preferred timeline.

After a dozen or so calls, I got another call from Adam. He has been my business partner for 26 years and is an exceptional CEO, with real dexterity in balancing the visionary and the operational. He was alarmed by the phone calls I was making.

"You need to stop scaring people," he said. His pushback was necessary. Scaring people would freeze them, when what I wanted was for them to move. So I tempered the message.

I said, "Meet me in the middle, and let's just scare them a little bit."

My focus shifted toward the opportunities unlocked by action, while keeping the dangers of inaction in view. I was not perfect in that calibration. At times, I leaned too far toward urgency and pushed harder than I would have liked to get leaders to engage with my message.

For several weeks, I made multiple calls per day. I started with the people I trusted most, the ones I knew could hear a hard message and act on it. I walked them through my app and showed them the data it had produced. I shared how I was using AI in my own day-to-day.

Some leaders got it immediately. They had been dabbling already and were waiting for permission to lean in. Their activation was swift, and soon they were emailing me about what they had built and new insights they had discovered.

Other leaders needed time. They listened and expressed interest, then went back to running their business as before. A few pushed back.

I noticed a pattern with the pushback. It mostly came from senior leaders whose careers had grown around a niche skill set. They had yet to process how the value of their expertise was about to be reconfigured. They weren't denying the relevance of AI to their work, but it seemed to me that many leaders thought AI was a bigger problem for entry-level workers and would be solved by someone else at a later time.

Pride carries people through twenty years of building a practice. At the higher tiers of leadership, in the middle of a major industry inflection point, pride can be a liability. To get the best out of an organization's AI transformation, leaders must be willing to accept that the ways they've been operating for the past two decades will change completely in the coming months. That is not easy to accept.

When it came to AI adoption, frontline workers were ahead of many senior leaders. That gap bothered me. A firm in which customer-facing workers ask for more while the leadership tier hesitates loses its best people first. Activation is more profound when it comes from the top.

There is a first-mover advantage at play here. Organizations that build AI infrastructure and training will hold an advantage that is hard to replicate. Specialists who lean into this evolution can offer clients far more value than they may have ever imagined. The leaders above them have to move first.

Using the right framework to drive AI transformation will build some of the most remarkable companies this industry has ever seen.

OneDigital intends to be one of those companies.

A New Framework for a New Era

What is the right framework for AI transformation?

Again, AI transformation is a talent management problem. For a generation, Human Capital Management (HCM) has been the lens through which organizations think about their people. The textbook definition is fairly stable across the discipline. HCM is the set of practices an organization uses to acquire, deploy, develop, compensate, and retain its workforce, with the underlying premise that the workforce is the sum of the humans on the payroll and that the management challenge is allocating dollars among those humans to maximize the value they produce.

HCM accurately describes what most firms have been doing since the 1990s. As an organizing framework for the next decade, though, the model carries a structural flaw. It's hiding in plain sight. It's the "H."

The HCM framework rests on the assumption that an organization's talent consists solely of humans. With artificial intelligence, that changes. Talent in a modern organization comprises humans and AI working together.

The challenges for traditional HCM go beyond adding AI agents alongside humans on the org chart. Organizations used to ask, "How many people do we need to accomplish a task?" This is the wrong question. A framework that begins by counting humans cannot describe, let alone manage, an organization whose capability comes from the integration of human and machine intelligence.

With AI augmentation, any human knowledge worker asking the right questions can do the work of an entire team. The new measurement is the intelligence powering the work. Today's question reads, **"What intelligence does our organization require, and how do we compose it?"**

By the time I asked this question out loud, Vinay and the team had been building toward an answer at OneDigital for more than two years. What we did next was give that work a name, a framework, and a sense of urgency. We surfaced a framework that applies to every employer of meaningful size in every white-collar industry facing the same disruption. We believe this same framework may also be applicable to gray- and blue-collar work as robotic technology advances.

Our framework is based on the following three assumptions: First, artificial intelligence is a new kind of talent to manage and integrate into your organization's work. Second, software deployment frameworks lack what AI transformation requires. Third, the people best equipped to lead this integration are your people leaders. These are your Chief Human Resources Officers (CHROs) or Chief People Officers (CPOs), the executives who already know how to hire, onboard, supervise, and develop human employees.

Future chapters will dismantle obstructive mental models, equip you with the right language for your organization's change management, and provide your change leaders with the framework we use at OneDigital to drive AI transformation. You will see how we moved from an efficiency lens to a talent-focused lens and what changed as a result. You will also meet the people inside our organization who made the work possible, those who struggled, and the mistakes we made along the way.

The window to do AI transformation right is open, and it will not stay open long. Your moment for action has arrived. This is your radiating red dot. The pages ahead carry the information you need to **move**.

2

Managing Your Entire Workforce

On a Tuesday afternoon, somewhere between the third and fourth hour of a Zoom call, I leaned back and said something that made Vinay pause.

> *"I think we've been measuring the wrong thing for years."*

He asked what I meant.

> *"We measure the workforce by what it costs and what it produces. Headcount. Compensation. Turnover. Productivity per employee. All of it measures the human workforce as if humans were the only kind of workforce. That has not been true for a while now. We just haven't updated how we think or what we measure."*

He sat with that for a moment, and then asked, "So, what are we really managing, if we're honest about what the workforce looks like today?"

I thought about it and said, "A team. A blended team. Some human, some digital. We have sophisticated tools for managing the human side and almost nothing coherent for managing the relationship between the two."

The concept brief that emerged from that conversation was sent to three people within OneDigital whose feedback we trusted. Keith Falk, our Managing Principal in Irvine, has clients in front of him every day. Meagan Karry leads our HR consulting practice out of Atlanta and is responsible for growing its revenue and capability. Elizabeth Chrane, also in Atlanta, is our Chief People Officer, and she would eventually be the one turning the framework on paper into a daily reality for 6,000 employees. Each of the three pushed us to think harder about the problem we were trying to solve.

None of the three were starting from scratch. By the time the concept brief reached them, OneDigital was more than two years into its AI journey. The Coworker program was live, our frontline consultants and advisors had been using AI in client work for some time, and we had built procurement, supervision, and training scaffolding around it. An early version of what would become Workforce Intelligence was already taking shape in how Elizabeth was running the people function and in how our work was being redesigned. What my all-nighter did was raise the stakes. The phone calls I made to senior leaders created a sense of urgency we had not yet generated from the inside. The Workforce Intelligence framework gave the work we were already doing a shared name, a common vocabulary, and a clear destination.

Keith and the Story of Workforce Management

Keith Falk is the right person to walk through the arc that built modern HR. He has watched the discipline evolve from the inside for thirty years and can describe its evolution in ten minutes.

For most of the twentieth century, the function we now call HR was Personnel Administration. Personnel handled payroll, compliance, headcount tracking, leave, and benefits. The head of Personnel reported to a senior administrator. The function did not have a seat at the executive table because Personnel's responsibilities were operational, not strategic.

The shift from Personnel to Human Capital Management began in the 1970s and was largely complete by the early 2000s. A generation of executives recognized that the operational framing of Personnel was inadequate for the future of work. Knowledge work was becoming the dominant form of work in developed economies, and the firms that recruited, developed, and retained their people most effectively would produce measurably superior results.

HCM did not throw Personnel out, but absorbed its responsibilities and added a strategic layer on top. This included workforce planning, talent management, succession planning, organizational development, and total rewards strategy. By 2010, every scaled organization had a CHRO or CPO and an HCM strategy. Firms without them operated at a structural disadvantage in the war for talent.

Gallup's research on employee engagement shows what HCM can produce when leaders take it seriously. As of 2024, only 31 percent of U.S. employees reported feeling engaged at work, the lowest level in a decade, and 70 percent of the variance in team engagement traced back to the quality of the manager.[1] Firms that took HCM seriously and invested in the practices the framework recommended produced measurably better outcomes for two decades running.

Keith points out that practitioners contested the shift from Personnel to HCM at every step. For decades, executives argued that the people function was a cost center and that elevating it to the C-suite was a fad. Those arguments are now awkward. No serious firm runs without HCM today. Except HCM must now change again.

We are entering an era of work in which the knowledge work HCM manages is no longer confined to human workers. So the next evolution of HCM will absorb it in the same way it absorbed Personnel. From payroll and compliance to hiring, development, performance management, and the architecture of total rewards, the disciplines HCM built around the human workforce are not going anywhere. They are the foundation for a new layer of management discipline.

What HCM brought to Personnel was a worldview that treated people as assets to develop and the talent function as a strategic discipline. The next layer brings its own worldview, anchored in the recognition that talent now includes the digital coworker working alongside the human one. Human capability today is joined by machine capability, and together they produce the organization's true work.

The worldview HCM rests on, that the value of an organization equals the sum of what its humans can do, was correct for as long as the workforce was composed entirely of humans. The composition has changed. The discipline that managed the human-only workforce is not sufficient to manage the workforce emerging in its place.

So what is this new stage of management called? It's called Workforce Intelligence. This is the layer above HCM, just as HCM is the layer above Personnel.

An organization's intelligence used to be inseparable from its human carriers. The advisor who formed the recommendation also drafted the memo. The underwriter who assessed the risk also produced the documentation. Org charts assumed bundling because no other arrangement was possible. AI breaks the bundle. Intelligence and the capability to act on it are now independently configurable, and that single structural change is the one for which HCM has no instrument. HCM organized itself around managing the carriers. The new discipline organizes itself around the cargo, who else carries it now, and how the whole composition produces the firm's results.

In most organizations today, software processes invoices without human involvement. Tools draft communications for a human to review and send. Platforms strategize on organizational data and offer recommendations for a manager to act on. AI agents are operating with increasing autonomy throughout the day's work, performing functions that a human used to handle at every step.

Those systems are performing the organization's work, producing its outputs, and generating its results. Each fits the operational definition of a coworker, but none are working under an official management system. Their human partners are still managed by HCM, but there is no management tier at the same level responsible for the AI workers.

And yet, digital coworkers have procurement, IT governance, software contracts, and renewal cycles. Why do they not have a management philosophy? There must be a framework that measures their contribution relative to the humans working alongside them, and whether that relationship is improving over time.

The misalignment between today's workforce and the framework leaders use to manage it is what causes most AI investments to fall short of expectations. Most organizations that have invested in AI have acquired the capability without a management strategy, not through negligence but due to the absence of a framework. They have the HCM playbook for their human workforce, but no equivalent for their digital workforce.

Vinay and I first tested our Workforce Intelligence framing with Keith. He pushed back, the way good practitioners always do. Unsurprisingly, our first iteration had some holes.

Our first error was to leave HCM's obsessive focus on headcount unaddressed. Keith zeroed in on this gap. He said, "Headcount is the metric that leaders rely on the most, but tells them the least. It's a vanity metric."

According to Keith, headcount tells you how many humans you are paying, and little more. It does not tell you what your organization is capable of doing, how quickly the firm can adapt, or how dense its skill base is relative to the work it performs.

When Keith wants to make a point, he reaches for Michael Lewis. The point he made about HCM was the main takeaway from Lewis's book *Moneyball*, which tells the story of how the wrong scouting metrics in baseball produced inferior results to a modernized framework. In *Moneyball*, the old baseball scouting model measured what scouts could see with their eyes: how a player looked, stood, swung, threw, and ran. The new model, designed by Billy Beane of the Oakland A's, focused on pure data. They looked at a player's on-base percentage, runs created, and little else. These were data that everyone had access to, but nobody focused on for fear of deviating from the norm. But when Beane's Oakland A's had winning percentages comparable to the

New York Yankees, and on a fraction of the budget, the league was forced to take notice.

HCM, Keith says, is in its Moneyball moment. Headcount is the bat-and-the-swing of workforce measurement. Firms that figure out what predicts winning will lap the firms that do not.

What predicts winning is a firm's capacity to adapt, and the density of its skill base relative to the work the organization performs. Neither of these can be measured by a payroll register. Both require a framework, which is the next layer of the HCM stack.

The stack has three layers. The bottom layer is what HCM traditionally covers. Pay people correctly, cover them with health insurance, build a retirement program that lets them plan, hire with rigor, and stay compliant with the law. This is the infrastructure layer of HCM. When it runs well, it is invisible. When it runs poorly, it drags down everything else in the management stack.

The middle layer is modern, strategic HR. This is the work most CPOs spend most of their time on: talent management, leadership development, culture work, and organizational design. The middle layer has more intangibles than its base layer, but is arguably more impactful on building an organization's capabilities. When first designed about 15 years ago, this layer gave early adopters a competitive edge. Since then, the tools for strategic HR have become widely accessible, making any HR-based competitive advantage harder to sustain.

The top layer of the stack is Workforce Intelligence (WI). This is the organization's designed capacity to compose and continuously improve the blended system of human and digital coworkers. WI measures the system's overall output and manages it for higher performance over time. Almost no organization is operating deliberately at the top layer of Workforce Intelligence yet.

Standard HCM asks whether the firm has the right people, pays them correctly, adequately covers them, and retains them long enough to achieve an adequate return on investment. Workforce Intelligence asks whether the firm's blended workforce, human and digital coworkers together, is becoming measurably more capable each quarter. One is a hygiene question with a forty-year-old playbook. The other is a strategic question almost no firm is currently asking.

When Vinay tested an early version of the stack with one of Adam Bruckman's YPO groups (Young Presidents' Organization; a cohort of CEOs that Adam has been meeting with for decades), one of the CEOs in the room made an interesting comment:

"Workforce Intelligence is sort of like succession planning."

Vinay agreed. Succession planning is already the exercise of identifying where capabilities and intelligence live within an organization and ensuring that if someone leaves or retires, the organization can sustain itself. The Workforce Intelligence question is how to do the same mapping with AI in the picture: where intelligence lives in humans, where it lives in AI, and how the relationship between the two represents what the firm is capable of doing today.

The CEO's framing was useful. Suddenly, a new concept like WI, which had sounded abstract, was anchored in a practice every executive in the room had already done. Leaders know how to identify where intelligence lives in their organizations. They know how to plan for what happens when intelligence leaves. The Workforce Intelligence move extends the practice to include a new source of intelligence in the mapping. The activity is not foreign. The scope has expanded.

Some thinkers have already moved past the HCM frame. Ravin Jesuthasan, whose research on the skills-powered organization examines how AI changes workforce planning, argues that the job is no longer the right unit for organizing work. The right unit, in his formulation, is the skill. Organizations move from counting jobholders to managing skills, treating each person as an evolving bundle of capabilities. The shift from job to skill is real progress over HCM, and the research behind it is rigorous.[2]

Workforce Intelligence parts ways with the skills frame because of what AI is now capable of doing. A skill is something discrete and trainable, like Excel modeling or the pulling of a benchmarking report. When you list the skills an advisor brings to a client, you have described the visible portion of their work. The judgment to know which question the client is really asking sits above the visible portion. So does the synthesis of a market trend and a regulatory shift into one coherent recommendation, alongside the read of a room that lets the person slow down when someone is afraid. These capacities constitute what we mean by intelligence.

Until recently, that level of work was unambiguously human, which is why a skills-only frame could function for a long time. The current generation of AI is operating in synthesis and pattern recognition, the territory the skills framework had implicitly walled off as irreducibly human. Once AI crosses into that territory, the skill stops being the right unit of analysis. The workforce is best described by the intelligence it can compose across humans and machines together. The move is from skills to intelligence.

Meagan and Elizabeth: Tangible Metrics and What Comes Monday

> *"The problem with most strategic frameworks is that they're descriptive without being measurable. They tell you what to think about. They don't tell you where you stand. We have to be able to measure WI for ourselves and for our clients."*

Vinay said this on a team Zoom call, and he is right. The absence of a number is the reason so many compelling ideas in management never change organizational behavior. Organizations manage what they measure.

Meagan's response to the concept brief is one of the most useful pieces of pushback I have received on any idea in my career. She read the brief carefully, found it interesting, and asked the question that needed to be asked.

> *"Is this real, or is it a relabeling of what good leaders have always done? Smart organizations have always thought carefully about how to deploy their people. They have always asked where capability should sit and how to build more of it. What, exactly, is new here, and is the new name necessary, or would the underlying shift happen regardless of what we called it?"*

I sat with that for longer than I wanted to. She was effectively asking, "What gives us the right to plant our flag on this framework? Is this actually novel, or is this a branding strategy?" It was a fair question.

Why does naming matter to a leader sitting inside their own firm, with their own pressures, and their own team? Naming has always mattered in business. The vocabulary used to describe a workforce determines what the firm measures. The measurements determine what leaders reward. The rewards determine how people behave. How people behave is, in the end, what the organization is.

Take the language a CPO inherits. HCM tells the CPO that their job is to manage 600 people, and to focus on metrics such as cost per person, productivity per person, turnover among people, and engagement scores. The dashboard reflects the vocabulary used during the quarterly conversation with the CEO. When revenue softens, the CPO often reaches for the only lever in their vocabulary: headcount.

The Workforce Intelligence framework includes various metrics and offers distinct levers. Rather than ask the CPO how many humans are needed to get the same outputs, the CPO is asked how intelligence is organized so that humans and AI Coworkers can maximize outputs. The same CPO, working under the same pressures, ends up making different decisions because the vocabulary made different levers visible.

The reason naming matters in your firm comes back to the daily decisions leaders make when nobody is watching. The vocabulary on the dashboard becomes the menu of options from which a leader picks. If you change the vocabulary, then you change the menu. However, a vocabulary that changes decisions still has to be attached to a number. Otherwise, the framework becomes a more sophisticated way of having the same conversation. This was also, effectively, what Elizabeth noted in her feedback.

Elizabeth Chrane, OneDigital's CPO, read the same concept brief as Keith and Meagan. Her response had two parts, both of which were useful.

The first concerned durability. HCM survived the move from on-premises HRIS (Human Resource Information System) to cloud HRIS to mobile-first platforms because the underlying discipline was about people, and it outlived every shift in the software stack beneath it. Workforce Intelligence has to clear the same bar. The structural shift must outlive the tools. If not, the tools would date the discipline within five years.

Vinay addresses WI's durability concerns in later chapters, when he discusses AI-agnostic systems and owning your intelligence.

The second part of Elizabeth's response was entirely pragmatic:

> *"I frequently read smart, forward-looking pieces like this and find myself nodding along with the premise and then thinking, okay, now what do I do with that on Monday?"*

This aligned with Meagan's feedback. Organizations don't need a new philosophical framework. They need new metrics. Only when leadership teams measure something new will behavioral change permeate the organization. So, what is the new metric, how can it be calculated, and what does it mean?

We designed a formula to identify the metric, which we call the Workforce Intelligence Score (WI Score). The formula is simple enough that a CEO can explain it in an elevator. When a CEO calculates their WI Score, they calculate it against the actual performance of organizations facing the same workforce composition challenge the CEO does.

A CEO who learns their firm sits in the bottom quartile of their industry does not need a consultant to tell them the firm has a problem. The formula is constructed so that the CEO can defend the imperative for change to their board with data. The CEO can identify the variable dragging down the score and direct resources to the specific problem rather than to a broad and expensive transformation initiative.

The repositioning of the people function within the firm is potentially the most significant in a generation. A CPO can now walk into a strategy session with a WI Score as a benchmark comparison tool, a productivity metric that translates workforce performance into the language CEOs and CFOs already speak, a number that sits comfortably next to EBITDA on the same slide.

The next chapter shows how to calculate the score, what it measures, and how a leader can act on it on Monday.

A note before the operational chapter that follows. Human relationships matter, and the relationships will continue to matter. The premise of Workforce Intelligence is that an integrated human-AI workforce produces better long-term outcomes precisely because it preserves the human capacities AI cannot replicate. This includes empathy, trust, the ability to read an eye roll across a conference table, and the judgment that comes from sitting next to someone, understanding what that person is afraid of, and knowing what they need to hear.

The benefits consultant who has earned a client's trust over fifteen years of showing up at the moments that mattered most holds a form of intelligence no AI model will replicate. The retirement advisor who sat with a recently widowed client and helped her see that she would be okay was performing work that is irreducibly human, and it will remain so for as long as people seek guidance from one another in moments of vulnerability.

There is a deeper reason human intelligence will remain central to this work, beyond the obvious one of relational warmth. Human intelligence is not finite. It evolves in ways no training set anticipates, generates connections no model could produce, and carries the dimensions of conscience, lived experience, and moral weight that an algorithm cannot access. AI, however powerful, is bound by its training data and the statistical distributions within it. Human intelligence is unbounded in ways that matter for the work most organizations do, because the questions clients and colleagues ask are rarely ones a model has seen before in exactly that form.

Workforce Intelligence does not diminish human contribution. The discipline clarifies where human value lives and protects it. A firm that continues to define the job of its advisors and consultants in terms of the analytical work that AI now performs faster and more cheaply will see its value erode in the not-so-distant future. The redefinition that protects human roles anchors the work in judgment, empathy, and the relationship layer that has not been factored out to an AI model.

Many organizations already have digital coworkers. Most are not managing them. Workforce Intelligence is the discipline of management work, and the next chapter is where measurement begins.

3

The Workforce Intelligence Score

Elizabeth Chrane's question hung over us for weeks:

"Okay, now what do I do with that on Monday?"

Our concept brief explained why Workforce Intelligence belonged above HCM, named the structural shift our firm was navigating, and gave the people function a new vocabulary for the next decade of work. The brief had not given Elizabeth a number. Without a number, the brief was a worldview waiting on an instrument, and Elizabeth was being asked, every quarter, to provide the CEO with something he could give to the board.

We needed a measurement instrument that worked within her timeline, used her existing data, and survived the CEO's or CFO's first follow-up question. We owed her that before we owed her any other deliverable.

The design work took six weeks.

Vinay and I worked from a few design rules before sketching the first version of the formula. The instrument had to run on data the firm had easily on hand. A measurement requiring new infrastructure or a new vendor would be dead before any CPO could put it in front of a board, which ruled out half the frameworks Vinay and I had been admiring. The signal also needed to move meaningfully when the workforce became more intelligent, since a number drifting within a 2 percent band, regardless of what the firm did with AI, would tell a leader little about whether their investments were working.

There was also a thematic requirement. AI transformation is a talent management problem, and an instrument that reads like a financial model would steer the conversation back outside the CPO's office to the finance and technical teams already vying for responsibility. Whatever Vinay and I built, the math had to be grounded in metrics that Elizabeth and her team could own.

The first version of the formula we sketched broke all of our design rules. We factored in changes to revenue, cost per employee, AI investment costs, and other year-over-year changes.

After weeks of pressure-testing and adjusting, we crossed out the formula and started over.

The temptation was to build a richer version of the productivity ratios every firm already runs. Revenue divided by headcount. Output per dollar of labor. The familiar shapes. We started there and walked away within an afternoon, because a productivity ratio cannot answer the question that Workforce Intelligence is asking.

A productivity ratio can rise on inputs that have no relationship to WI. A firm can lay off 20 percent of its workforce on a Friday and watch its revenue-per-employee number climb the following Monday. The number rose because the denominator fell. The remaining workforce did not change in any observable way during the seventy-two hours between those two readings. The ratio cannot distinguish between a firm that got smaller and one that became more capable.

The same dynamic shows up when a firm raises prices, when accounting choices reclassify contractors as employees of an outsourcing vendor, or when a single business line spins off and exits the denominator. Every one of those moves improves a productivity ratio. None of them is evidence of a workforce that has built a better working relationship with AI.

Workforce Intelligence needed to measure a different signal.

The Signal Is Behavioral

Workers seem to be split on how they should collaborate with AI. In 2025, Microsoft surveyed over 30,000 knowledge workers around the globe to ask how they used AI in their work.[1] About half described AI as a command-based tool. A worker in the command-mode population issued a request, accepted AI's response, and closed the session. The other half described AI as a thought partner. A worker in the thought-partner population pushed back on the outputs, fed context into the ongoing exchange, and used the conversation to sharpen the question they were trying to answer.

The even split was unexpected, but the more important insight came on further investigation. When Microsoft segmented the firms in the survey by performance, the top-performing organizations were the ones whose workers had moved decisively toward the thought-partner side. The cognitive shift from command mode to collaborative use was the behavior that correlated with the financial outcomes leaders were chasing.

The behavioral shift sits upstream of the financial outcome. The shift itself is what every firm chasing real returns on AI investment needs. An instrument that does not measure this behavioral shift cannot accurately measure Workforce Intelligence.

The instrument we built is based on a single, multiple-choice survey question:

> **"When you use AI at work, which best describes you or your workforce?"**

The respondent picks one of five options. Each option carries a numerical weight that we ran against the Microsoft data before locking the scale in place.

Factor (A)	Workforce description
0.12	We do not use AI, or very few employees do.
0.28	Most employees ask AI questions and use the answers (transactional use).
0.55	Many employees work through problems with AI in multi-turn exchanges (iterative use).
0.82	A significant proportion say they cannot imagine working without AI (collaborative use).
1.00	AI Coworkers operate as genuine team members; the workforce is fully blended.

The percentage of employees in each tier, multiplied by the tier's weight and summed across the five tiers, produces a single number between 0.12 and 1.00. We call that number the AI Amplification Factor, or variable A.

Variable A is dimensionless and reads on a clean 0-to-1 scale that a CPO can interpret at a glance. Adding the collaboration question to whatever pulse instrument the firm already runs produces variable A in an afternoon. The setup adds no new vendors or infrastructure. One well-placed question does the work.

A workforce evenly split across the iterative and collaborative tiers produces an A in the high 0.60s. A workforce stuck almost entirely in transactional use produces an A near 0.28. A workforce that has reached genuine co-intelligence sits close to 1.00. The number tells a leader where their firm sits on the only behavioral spectrum that matters for AI transformation, and the spectrum is the one that the world's largest workplace surveys have already shown to predict financial outcomes.

A company's AI Amplification Factor does not respond to the financial maneuvers that move other productivity ratios. The 20 percent layoff that improves revenue per employee leaves the factor unchanged, because the workers who remain answer the collaboration question the same way they did before their colleagues left. Price increases leave variable A undisturbed, and so do contractor reclassifications and one-time accounting restructures. The factor moves only when the people in the workforce change how they relate to AI in their daily work.

The CFO who runs the firm's financial dashboard cannot influence variable A from their desk. The variable sits outside their toolkit on purpose. Robert Kaplan and David Norton made the argument in 1992 in the *Harvard Business Review* that nonfinancial leading indicators, anchored in an explicit causal chain to financial outcomes, are the variables that predict where a business is going rather than report where it has been.[2] This factor is exactly that kind of variable.

Variable A also accounts for the fact that Workforce Intelligence is a talent shift. This makes the AI Amplification Factor a talent measurement metric. The number rises when leaders coach, redesign workflows around AI collaboration, model the behavior themselves, and hold their teams accountable for moving from transactional to thought-partner use.

This doesn't mean variable A belongs solely to the people officers.

Every firm has a productivity metric that the leadership team reviews on a slide. The metric varies by industry. A professional services firm reads billable hours per practitioner. A software company reads revenue per employee. An insurance firm reads plans renewed per advisor or contracts written per underwriter. A manufacturing company reads the contribution margin per full-time employee. Whatever the chosen metric, the leadership team has already agreed on its definition, the finance team already pulls it on a quarterly cadence, and the CFO has already defended it to the board at least once. The metric has passed its elevator pitch.

The Workforce Intelligence Score is the firm's existing productivity metric, multiplied by A. This approximates the correlation between AI transformation and the metrics that matter most to the executive team. The firm's productivity output is effectively weighted by the cognitive process the workforce used to produce it.

A firm with a strong productivity metric and an AI Amplification Factor near 0.28 is producing its results with a workforce that treats AI as a vending machine. The same productivity numbers paired with a variable A in the high 0.70s describe a firm compounding intelligence into the workforce that produced them. The two firms look identical on a conventional productivity slide. The score separates them. See

Figure 3.1 for the full formula and the AI Amplification Factor tier weights.

The score offers insight into where the firm's productivity is headed, not only where it is now.

The structural justification for multiplication traces back to Robert Solow's 1957 paper on technical change and the aggregate production function. Solow showed that productivity

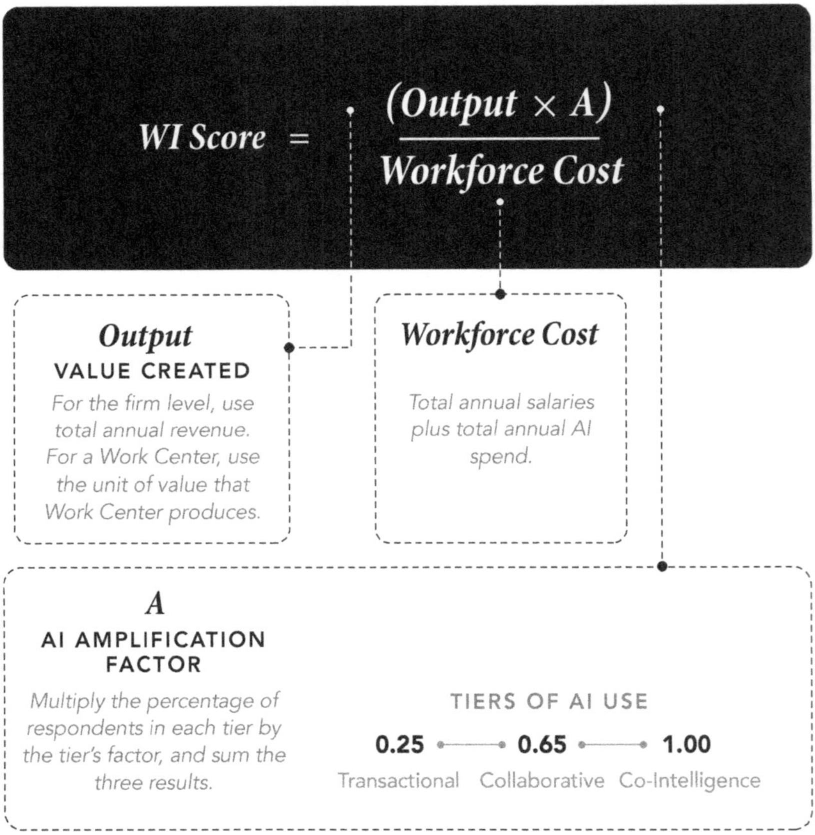

Figure 3.1 The Workforce Intelligence Score formula. Value Created (Output) multiplied by the AI Amplification Factor (A), divided by total Workforce Cost (annual salaries plus annual AI spend). A is calculated by surveying the workforce across three tiers of AI use—Transactional (weight 0.25), Collaborative (weight 0.65), and Co-Intelligence (weight 1.00)—multiplying the percentage of respondents in each tier by the tier's weight and summing the three results.

inputs interact multiplicatively, which is to say a strong technology factor cannot compensate for a weak labor factor by simple arithmetic.[3] The Workforce Intelligence Score borrows the structural logic and replaces Solow's economy-level variables with two measurements any employer can pull in an afternoon. The score changes substantially only when the firm's productivity metric and its collaborative AI behavior move together.

A CPO carrying the score into a quarterly review carries one number. The number sits next to EBITDA on the slide, and the math behind it is the firm's own productivity metric multiplied by a variable her CFO doesn't manage.

Finally, we had a metric Elizabeth could use. Now we just had to make sure it could stand up to scrutiny.

The J-Curve

The hard question every CFO asks at this point in the conversation is this:

> *"I have doubled our AI spend over the past 18 months, and our productivity metric has barely moved. How do I read the new AI score during a year like that?"*

A reality of doing AI transformation right is that the short-term numbers will not support the initiative. In fact, any serious AI program documenting economic growth will see patterns that seem to suggest the program is failing. Thankfully, this pattern has already been researched.

It's called the J-Curve.

In 2021, economists Erik Brynjolfsson, Daniel Rock, and Chad Syverson described the Productivity J-Curve in the *American Economic Journal: Macroeconomics*.[4] When mapping investment in a major technology initiative like AI against productivity gains (with total investment over time on the x-axis and productivity gains on the y-axis) the curve looks like the letter J. This is because general-purpose technologies like AI require complementary investments before they produce measurable productivity gains. Process redesign, workforce retraining, coworker development, and organizational restructuring are all expensed rather than capitalized under standard accounting, and the expense is recognized on the income statement during the years the new capability is being built. Measured productivity dips during that time as the workforce adjusts to the new technology, and then rises starkly in the years that follow.

Measuring variable A will help leaders accurately predict whether their AI transformation will turn productivity gains upward during the initial trough. If variable A remains unchanged, then the trough is a cause for alarm. That means productivity gains are declining, with no indication that the company's behavior toward AI is shifting in a positive direction. However, if variable A is increasing, the company can reason that the J-Curve pattern will materialize if it stays the course.

This just leaves the matter of communicating the actual variable A numbers more clearly.

Reading the Score in Four Bands

The score reads naturally into four bands: Lagging, Developing, Performing, and Leading.

Lagging firms have a workforce stuck almost entirely in transactional use of AI. The score (0.12–0.28) is well below the firm's industry median, and its competitive position is eroding even when the income statement appears acceptable.

Developing firms have started moving the workforce into iterative use. The score (0.28–0.55) is finally climbing off the floor. Most of the AI work happens in isolated pockets across the firm, but the leadership team is doing the early work of broadening the practice.

Performing firms have moved a critical mass of the workforce into collaborative use of AI. The score (0.55–0.82) falls in the upper half of the firm's industry distribution, and quarterly improvements appear in both the productivity metric and variable A.

Leading firms are at the top. The score (0.82–1.00) reflects genuine co-intelligence across most of the workforce, and the firm's competitors are watching the competitive gap widen by the quarter.

The bands work best for within-industry comparison and for tracking a firm against itself over time. Absolute scores across industries require segment benchmarking, which the annual OneDigital Workforce Intelligence Trends Report will publish as the benchmark dataset matures.

The Workforce Intelligence Score gives a leader a position and a direction. The score reports where the firm sits on the behavioral spectrum that predicts financial returns on AI and where the trajectory is heading from quarter to quarter.

The score does not move on its own, though. Variable A only improves when the people in the workforce change how they work with AI. This calls for two paradigm shifts, one at the individual level and one at the enterprise level. The chapters that follow describe both shifts.

4

The First Paradigm Shift: Transactional to Collaborative

VARIABLE A ONLY moves when the workers themselves change how they work with AI, and the change happens one mind at a time. A leader looking at a flat AI Amplification Factor trend across their workforce cannot lift the number by purchasing more licenses or scheduling another training session. The first paradigm shift is psychological before it is technical.

Workers need to stop thinking about AI like an information vending machine. It's not a more social version of Google Search Engine. AI is a thinking partner. The three tiers of AI use, and the kinds of prompts that distinguish them, are shown in Figure 4.1.

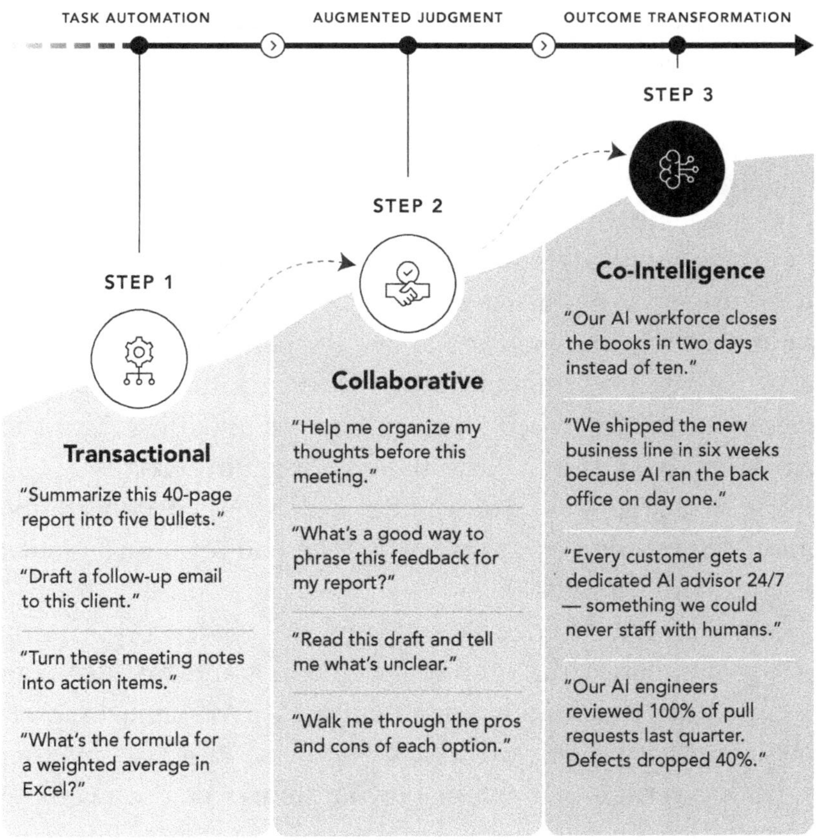

Figure 4.1 The three tiers of AI use—Transactional, Collaborative, and Co-Intelligence—shown with representative employee prompts at each tier. Examples are illustrative and not drawn from a specific deployment.

A workforce that completes this first paradigm shift will move variable A above 0.28.

I spend a significant portion of each week in conversations with executives across the industries OneDigital serves. Whenever the subject of AI comes up and I ask what their firm is doing with it, the answer that comes back is almost always some version of the same five words:

"Oh yeah, we use Copilot."

I have heard that sentence so often I could set it to music.

Sometimes a qualifier follows, like a reference to ChatGPT, a summarization tool in the email client, or a built-in AI feature of the CRM. Whatever the qualifier, the underlying signal stays the same. The firm bought a tool, therefore the firm has handled the AI question.

It's a trademark attitude of the Lagging band of variable A.

Transactional AI has its place. For example, one evening before dinner, Vinay needed a recipe. A Google search would have meant ten links stacked above (or below) eight sponsored ads and a twelve-paragraph essay about a kitchen renovation buried over the ingredient list. Instead, he asked his AI for the recipe directly and got a clean ingredient list in seconds.

The exchange was faster than Google's and entirely transactional. Vinay ended up exactly where he had set out to go, with no detour and no surprise.

Transactional AI covers a wide range of office work. Drafting meeting summaries and summarizing memos are two easy examples. The work is real, and a fair amount of it saves time. However, time savings are limited to single tasks. This is highly convenient for the individual contributor but hardly moves the needle on enterprise-level productivity.

Remember, Microsoft's 2025 survey found that about half of workers who use AI at work use it transactionally.[1] What's interesting, though, is that the difference between those workers and the ones already using AI as a thought partner is not a skill gap. The difference is purely psychological.

Many of the same professionals who use AI transactionally at work are already using it collaboratively in their personal lives. At home, AI is their therapist, their fitness coach, their parenting sounding board, and more. They have extended AI chat threads that carry across sessions and build on accumulated context. And then those same people go to work the next day and ask Copilot to clean up a spreadsheet, summarize a document, and debug some code.

Reskilling won't address the dichotomy between these workers' at-work and at-home behaviors.

The good news is that it's unlikely firms will face a skills shortage for their AI transformation. Professionals who collaborate with AI at home and use AI transactionally at work already know *how* to extend a conversation and push back on an AI's output. So, what's stopping them from behaving that way at work?

There is actually a deep psychological barrier at play. It's called "authenticity concern." And the best man I know to describe and address this barrier is John Carew.

John Carew is a senior corporate development executive at OneDigital. He manages the M&A processes that have driven a decade-plus of inorganic growth at the firm. He is fifty-seven years old and has spent his career in a profession defined by relationships and high-stakes financial analysis.

John uses AI every day, and his use is the clearest illustration of the top variable A tier (Co-Intelligence 1.00) I have encountered.

John uses AI as a sparring partner for deal logic. He builds a full business case to do a deal and then constructs a competing case to walk away, pushing hard against both. He stress-tests each narrative and surfaces weaknesses in his own assumptions, challenging his position by posing it to an adversary with no stake in the outcome. The AI sharpens his judgment by forcing him to defend both sides of an argument before bringing it under the scrutiny of a committee.

When I asked whether AI has made him 50, 100, or 200 percent more productive, he pushed back on my framing. "The right frame," he says, "is capability expansion." AI has increased the scope and depth of his work. "It's less '200 percent more productive' and more 'I'm doing the work of a deal team, not just a deal person,'" he says.

John extends the same philosophy at home. He bought his wife, who works as an epidemiologist, a premium Google Gemini subscription and encouraged her to use it daily. Then he gave her the same instructions he's been giving each of his work peers: "Make yourself obsolete. The better you use AI, the more obsolete you as a data analyst will be, and the more valuable you as an epidemiologist will be. If you do that, you will never be obsolete."

The working partnership John has built with his AI gets richer the longer he collaborates with it. The outputs are unmistakably his because the artifacts hold his methodology and his point of view. Anyone else asking AI the same question would get a different answer, because the conversations John has been having with the AI for over a year have shaped his dialogue. Most senior professionals across our firm have not yet built a partnership like John's, and the cost of waiting compounds quarterly.

People are working with AI in their relationships and health, in financial decisions that used to require a paid advisor, and on creative projects they keep private. Most of them have never attempted the same kind of extended, iterative conversation in a professional setting. They go home at night and brainstorm with their AI, then come to work in the morning and don't collaborate with the technology beyond the boundaries of a Copilot subscription. Why?

This is where the authenticity concern comes in.

Many professionals carry a sincere discomfort with the idea that AI-assisted work is authentically theirs. They feel uneasy putting their name on an analysis the AI helped shape, and they hesitate to send a client proposal drafted through an AI conversation rather than composed in solitude. Collaborating with AI on their thinking feels like crossing the line from using a tool to relying on a crutch.

The feeling is that if the AI contributed to the idea, the idea is no longer fully theirs.

Or, to use John's words, they are afraid of making themselves obsolete at work.

The reluctance stems from a valid concern that if they offload the thinking they are paid to do, they become replaceable by technology that does the actual work. It's a fair instinct, but it stops short of the full picture. As John demonstrated, when you consult *with* the AI as it does the work, you become your own replacement. If anything, it allows you to do *more* of the thinking you are paid to do, because the AI can push and pull on ideas with you tirelessly until you have a refined conclusion or deliverable. And by that logic, the thinking is still yours.

Humans are a social species. Most of our best work happens in dialogue with other minds. The exchange of ideas and reactions generates the kind of unexpected connection a single mind in isolation rarely produces. AI can provide that exchange. The AI adapts to a professional's specific strengths and weaknesses, supplementing the areas where her depth runs thin. When done well, the conversation unlocks a level of thinking that person not reaching on their own.

No one else can reproduce the output of a real collaboration between you and AI, because each conversation is unique to the participants. A consultant's industry knowledge, their client roster, the judgment they developed over two decades of getting the work occasionally wrong, and all of their experiences shape the output as much as the AI does. Treating

AI-assisted work as less authentic than solo work ignores what collaboration with AI makes possible.

David Heinemeier Hansson, the creator of Ruby on Rails and CTO of 37signals, has described working this way as a kind of addictive feedback loop. When the gap between having an idea and seeing the idea realized compresses from weeks to hours, the temptation is to treat the moment like a limited-time opportunity and work until you collapse.[2] I experienced this myself on the night of the radiating red dot.

Collaborative AI use produces better outputs and a cognitive acceleration that is far more rewarding than the transactional approach. Unfortunately, a logical but misplaced sense of protectiveness prevents people from inviting AI to collaborate with them at work. How do we get over this fear?

There is a time to be gentle, and there is a time to rattle cages. The pattern we've been observing is that, once people start using AI collaboratively at work, they experience the benefits and the rewarding nature of the feedback loop first hand, and buy in. When they're at that stage, we can afford to be gentle. Until they are at that stage, shock has value.

There was one presentation that Vinay and Elizabeth Chrane gave about AI strategy that did not go as planned. They were walking through the vision and the deployment model that would carry it. The audience was OneDigital's most senior leaders, the people who would need to champion the work within their own divisions for our AI transformation to scale. We were trying to make the jump from the Lagging band (0.12-0.28) to the Developing one (0.28-0.55).

A veteran sales leader, whom I will call David, stood up and delivered blunt pushback. David did not see how any of the AI material related to how a senior sales leader actually closed business in the field. AI struck him as a back-office utility, fine for the people writing memos and summarizing reports, but less relevant the closer the work got to a client meeting or a deal in motion.

David had a strong track record of excellence in his field. Nobody would have questioned that. However, David was assuming that because AI would struggle to compete with his level of competence and expertise, the technology had nothing to offer him.

Vinay was equally blunt in his response. He told David, "You are at the top of your game right now with respect to sales. You are going to get lapped by a younger generation that is using this technology, and you need to step up."

The room was quiet.

David's pushback is common. From where he sat, AI was a tool for writing emails and summarizing documents, work that occupied a small fraction of his day and was not the source of his competitive advantage. The collaborative mode was invisible to him because no one had walked him through what the mode looked like in the context of his work. Still, that was no excuse for him not getting his hands dirty with the technology.

David needed to be told that he wouldn't be replaced by AI, but would be outperformed by other human workers collaborating with AI. He needed his cage rattled. Thankfully, when done with the right intent, rattling cages can get people to make the jump from Lagging to Developing.

The night my cage was rattled, with the radiating red dot, the calls I made were almost entirely to fellow leaders. The choice of audience was deliberate. OneDigital already had heavy AI usage in the field at that point. Our frontline workforce, the consultants, and account managers in regular client contact had all been working with AI for months. Many of them were ahead of where most leaders in our industry were at the time.

The activation moment needed to happen at the leadership tier above them. The practice heads and regional executives made decisions that would either accelerate the work the front line was doing or slow it down.

The calls ran six or eight a week for several weeks. The format was simple. I would get a fellow leader on a video call, share my screen, and walk through how I had been using AI, from issuing commands to working through problems alongside the system.

Some of those leaders got the message on the first call. Some leaders had even been dabbling in their personal lives, and thought they just needed permission to work collaboratively with AI in their work. These activations were quick, and within weeks I had senior leaders sending me notes about tools they had built and connections they had reached with the help of an AI partnership. They were moving through the Development band quickly.

Other leaders needed more time, and a little more force.

One of the calls I made was to Stan Bukowski. He leads our Medicare business, OneDigital Advanced Health, out of the Willis Tower in Chicago. He is in his mid-thirties and runs a $150 million operation with roughly 500 employees. His team handles 3,000 to 5,000 consumer calls every day during enrollment periods.

Stan built his career on the ability to read an industry and move quickly within it. He understands data and sales execution, and he had been using AI in his day-to-day work for months before I called him. By every surface measure, he was already doing the work.

On this call, I told Stan what Vinay and I had been seeing and where I believed the industry was headed. If his business did not move forward on a greater AI transformation, the business would fall behind. Across all of OneDigital's verticals, we had the opportunity to become the largest player in the consumer space before the broader market caught up. The opportunity would not wait for anyone.

We were not seeing any indicators of this development in the data. My call with Stan surfaced the reason.

It turned out that he had spent months operating the way most professionals do: transactionally. He asked AI questions and accepted its answers. AI summarized industry memos faster than he could on his own. CMS regulatory updates were processed by the AI in less time. Stan's work was useful and saved him small chunks of time throughout a busy week. But he and his team were not *collaborating* with AI.

I wanted Stan to collaborate with AI to help him think through the strategic trajectory of a $150 million Medicare operation. I wanted model scenarios for how CMS regulatory changes would ripple through his business over the next three to five years. That thinking was not present.

> "*Stan, this is not optional,*" I said. "*Wake up to what's happening, and start figuring out what you need to do, because what you're doing right now isn't good enough.*"

It was a bit of a gamble on my end to be so aggressive. Thankfully, it was the shock to his system that he needed.

After we hung up, Stan started mapping a plan immediately. He did not schedule a planning retreat or commission a strategy deck from his team. He broke his thinking into two categories: entry-level quick hits he could stand up in operations within days, and bigger-picture items that would take structured effort and dedicated resources. Then he began rethinking workflows he had been managing the same way for years.

As he worked, he realized that there was, in his own words, "another level to AI collaboration that I had not been tapping into."

One example captures the magnitude of what Stan was unearthing. His compliance team used to have thirty-five to forty people manually scoring recorded calls against regulatory standards, with each reviewer processing about seven calls a day. A second team audited the first, and a manager oversaw the auditors.

With a brilliant redesign that partnered his team with AI Coworkers, Stan's team now uploads 700 to 1,000 calls daily. Even more impressive is that the outputs are more accurate than the manual process ever was. The AI highlights specific moments in a call where an agent may have failed to read a required statement or phrased a response in a way that could trigger a CMS complaint. In those instances, the system even recommends alternate language.

Stan looked at the system, saw the results, and told his team they should train directly on the AI's recommendations rather than writing their own coaching materials. When I heard Stan say that, I realized his team had crossed from Lagging to Developing, and was nearing the Performing band. It wouldn't be long before his team was Leading.

I later learned that, a few days after our call, Stan sat down with one of his senior data analysts. The analyst had already given a presentation on AI to the team and had been mapping out ideas. When Stan met with the analyst and described how he was starting to treat AI differently, the expression on the analyst's face changed.

The analyst was already aware of OneDigital's AI efforts and had been following Vinay's work closely, so the shift in the room was not about new information. What was different was the leadership signal from Stan. The one-on-one signaled permission to the analyst to commit fully to AI transformation in his work.

A cascading effect took place in Stan's team. The analyst had been waiting despite working at a company that openly talked about AI. He had a hunch that his posture toward AI aligned with the company's, but he balked at taking action because he was unsure of his direct leadership.

When this became apparent, Stan, Vinay, and I realized something important about AI transformation: Activation must come from the top down.

Some on Stan's team were ready to lean in early, and there were others who pushed back. He was direct with people who pushed back. The work transformation was not going to be optional. This wasn't to dismiss all forms of pushback, though.

Stan described a conversation with one of his leaders, who said he got upset when a direct report sent a response that was clearly AI-generated. "This isn't them thinking," the leader told Stan. "This isn't what they sound like when they talk to me."

Stan admitted he used to share that view, used to feel protective of the line between human thought and machine-assisted output. His mind changed when he realized that AI collaboration expands a person's thinking rather than replaces it. AI opens up ideas and perspectives that might not come naturally to everyone, and AI can put a person on a more level playing field with colleagues who happen to have a natural advantage in speed or analytical ability. Stan reframed it for me on the call, and I have used the line in conversations with leaders ever since. AI works best as an equalizer and an amplifier, never as a substitute for the work of the mind.

Take inventory of yourself. Understand what you are good at, where you struggle, what you enjoy doing, and what you avoid. Then use AI to fill the gaps. A strategic thinker whose written memos always read flat can use AI to draft the prose version of an argument they have already worked out. Maybe it *is* better if you spend less time thinking about how to write emails.

OneDigital is not the only firm making the case for using AI collaboratively. In March 2026, Zapier, an online single-point automation and workflow service platform, published the second version of its AI Fluency Rubric, the framework it uses to evaluate every job candidate. Zapier had spent the prior year assessing every candidate against an initial fluency standard, and the lessons learned reshaped their understanding of AI fluency itself. The rebuilt rubric reached its conclusions independently of OneDigital's work, and they align almost exactly with the argument Vinay and I have been making.

Zapier's central finding after a year of testing is that the strongest indicator of AI fluency is iteration. A candidate who pushes back on an AI output and adapts the approach with each exchange has the fluency Zapier hires for, regardless of how many tools they list on their resume. Zapier cites Anthropic's AI Fluency Index research for the empirical anchor.[3]

To detect iteration at the candidate stage, Zapier rebuilt its skills tests to observe candidates working with AI in real time. The hiring team watches how candidates prompt AI and where they push back when the AI's first response is unsatisfactory. The company writes that a rough result with strong reasoning and visible iteration is a better signal than a polished result with no visible process behind it. If someone is not meaningfully improving their work with AI support, they do not meet the bar.

Zapier hires for the upper tiers of the AI Amplification Factor, not the lower, and is willing to invest the operational complexity required to tell potential hires apart.

It also added a manager-specific requirement that maps directly to Stan's story. A manager who is personally fluent but whose team still uses the old way does not meet the bar, even when the same fluency standard would clear an individual contributor. Zapier looks for managers who create psychological safety for experimentation, and who redesign workflows so that AI meaningfully changes how the team's work gets done. Stan walking into the meeting with his data analyst and signaling personal investment in the work was the same move Zapier has now codified as a hiring requirement for every new manager.

The outcome Zapier reports is significant. AI usage sits at 100 percent across the company, with every team having moved from personal experimentation to redesigning workflows around AI. The workforce-wide shift into the Co-Intelligence tier of variable A is the test case we were hoping someone outside our firm would run.

One additional point from Zapier reframes the authenticity concern in a useful way. With AI, the company writes, "You can delegate the work, but not the accountability." When collaborating with AI, human workers define what "good work" looks like. Humans are the ones responsible for evaluating every output against their own standards.

The paradigm shift from transactional to collaborative AI use occurs at the individual level. The change occurs in one person's mind, through their willingness to engage with AI as a thinking partner rather than as a search engine. The tools are already available. The work is to use the tools differently.

The authenticity concern is reasonable in light of the decades professionals have spent sharpening their thinking skills. But once people begin to iterate with AI as a thinking partner, more often than not they are hooked. At the leadership level, this has a cascading effect on AI transformation.

The moment a leader's team watches them fumble through their own clumsy prompts and produce work they could not have produced alone, the barriers begin to disintegrate.

In the language of the Workforce Intelligence Score, the first paradigm shift is about getting the organization out of the Lagging band (0.12-0.28) and into the Developing band (0.28-0.55).

To get into the upper two bands of AI transformation, the second paradigm shift is required. Hundreds of individuals collaborating brilliantly with their own AI in isolation does not produce an intelligent organization. The setup produces a hundred separate units of intelligence operating with no shared knowledge. Collective intelligence does not grow because individual intelligences are not connected.

Solving that problem, moving the collaborative shift from individual to enterprise, requires a different kind of work.

5

The Second Paradigm Shift: Individual to Enterprise AI Collaboration

A BENEFITS CONSULTANT in Charlotte spent forty-five minutes one Tuesday morning teaching her AI the nuances of a self-funded health plan for a manufacturing client. By Wednesday, a colleague in Denver was teaching his own AI the same lesson for a different client. Neither consultant knew the other one had done the work. Both of their AIs would archive the interaction as soon as the chat window closed.

The institutional knowledge that should have compounded from each conversation evaporated. OneDigital paid for the same lesson twice.

That Charlotte-Denver redundancy, multiplied across 6,000 consultants on the OneDigital roster, every year, in every line of business the firm operates, leaks AI lessons out of the firm faster than the firm can build them. Vinay and I believe a workforce operating that way actively erodes the firm's intellectual capital, because every AI conversation that goes unshared takes institutional knowledge with it when the chat window closes.

Individual collaboration alone delivers limited institutional benefit. The lessons each consultant learns through their personal AI rarely travel across the firm to the colleagues who would have used them. The second paradigm shift moves the firm from individual collaboration to enterprise collaboration, and most AI initiatives stall short of meaningful return on investment because they never make the jump.

In early April 2026, Vinay sent me a recording of a call he had with a client. He told me to watch the entire recording. In forty minutes, the recording surfaced nearly every organizational tension point involved in the enterprise-AI thesis.

The client was an HR leader, whom I will call Avery, head of human resources at the U.S. subsidiary of a European-headquartered industrial manufacturing group. The U.S. operation is based in the Southeast and has a workforce of roughly 300 administrative employees. Avery had been trying to move her organization toward AI adoption for months, with limited success. Our team set up the call as an informal conversation, a chance for Avery to ask questions and for Vinay to share how we had been approaching the problem at OneDigital.

Avery appeared on screen with a bright virtual office background. Her demeanor in the first few minutes was measured, and she picked her words carefully as she began to describe her situation.

The European parent operates a global enterprise HRIS system, and the U.S. operation runs on it. Locally, the U.S. operation runs its own payroll and workforce management platforms. The European parent is interested in AI but, in Avery's words, is "*very, very slow to react*." Adding a new component to the global system typically takes two years to roll out. Further, the corporate-approved AI chatbot is so restricted by IT security guardrails that employees are utilizing their own paid consumer AI subscriptions to collaborate with AI instead.

At least those employees were willing to adopt AI. The more Avery talked about the need to jump on AI transformation, the more a team of analysts at her U.S. operation pushed back. They said they use Python for data analysis and can set up automated reports that accomplish similar tasks. They thought an AI agent would be redundant.

To summarize Avery's problems, of the roughly 300 administrative employees at the U.S. operation, about 40 percent were already collaborating with AI. Some used the corporate-approved version, with many more working outside the company's security parameters on personally paid ChatGPT accounts. Avery had told them not to use the free version and to avoid entering sensitive data into any AI system, though enforcement was beyond her reach. She had no visibility into what information her employees were sharing with platforms her organization did not control.

And her company was building zero institutional knowledge from any of its AI work.

Avery's situation is, sadly, the norm. Microsoft and LinkedIn's 2024 Work Trend Index found that over three-quarters of AI users were bringing their own AI tools to work, a phenomenon the report labeled "Bring Your Own AI," or BYOAI.[1] The report flagged a striking gap between awareness and action, with nearly four of five leaders calling AI adoption critical to remaining competitive while only three of five conceded their organizations had built a plan for enterprise AI transformation.

The gap between leadership awareness and organizational action is the incubator for a dangerous phenomenon called "shadow AI."

AI unlocks productivity at the individual level, and every organization's best frontline workers are determined to get their hands on it. They are not waiting for corporate permission. Their managers have no visibility into much of this newfound productivity and no way to measure it. The shadow AI usage creates cause for alarm.

The security implications of shadow AI are a security officer's nightmare. When an employee pastes a client's financial data into a personal AI account, the platform provider can observe the data. When proprietary business processes or pricing models flow into consumer-grade AI tools, the organization loses control of its most sensitive intellectual property without any executive's awareness. Avery was aware, though, and so she told her frontline workers to be careful. She didn't tell them to stop because, in her assessment, telling 300 employees not to use the fastest-adopted technology in human history was unrealistic.

Vinay and I read Avery's reasoning as sound, given the circumstances.

When companies finally acknowledge the pervasiveness of shadow AI and initiate enterprise AI adoption, nine out of ten make AI an IT project. The CIO inherits ownership on a Tuesday morning, and by Friday, a platform evaluation is underway. Architecture and security reviews chew up the next two quarters.

Somewhere around month seven, a steering committee forms to assess which enterprise AI platform best fits the firm's existing technology stack at an acceptable cost.

The IT-led response checks every box a conservative executive under investor scrutiny wants checked in a new initiative, which is precisely why so many AI transformations launched this way die before they reach the workforce. Gartner's evidence on Microsoft Copilot tells the story.

A 2024 Digital Workplace survey of organizations trying out Microsoft 365 Copilot, the interface that lets users collaborate with a selection of AI engines inside the Microsoft suite, found the conversion rate to large-scale deployment was only 6 percent. Of the employees who received pilot access, most struggled to integrate the tool into their daily work. For nearly half of all users, engagement declined quickly after rollout.[2] One year later, a subsequent Gartner survey reported that the conversion rate had dropped to 5 percent.[3] This is the Copilot Plateau, shown in Figure 5.1.

Why are so many large-scale adoption efforts failing? One analysis of the survey explains it plainly. "Poor Copilot adoption is often caused by enterprise organizations treating it like a standard software rollout instead of a larger behavior change."[4]

The organizations that purchased licenses, connected them across their workplace applications, sent an announcement email, and expected productivity to rise had followed the playbook that worked for CRM rollouts, ERP deployments, collaboration platform launches, and every other enterprise software adoption of the prior three decades. The playbook stalls on contact with AI, because AI behaves like a colleague that needs a working relationship, and the design of working relationships sits well outside the IT department's traditional remit.

Of course, on the call with Vinay, Avery already knew all of this. About halfway through the call, Vinay asked her whether she wanted to include the sister subsidiaries in an initial assessment. Her response was immediate.

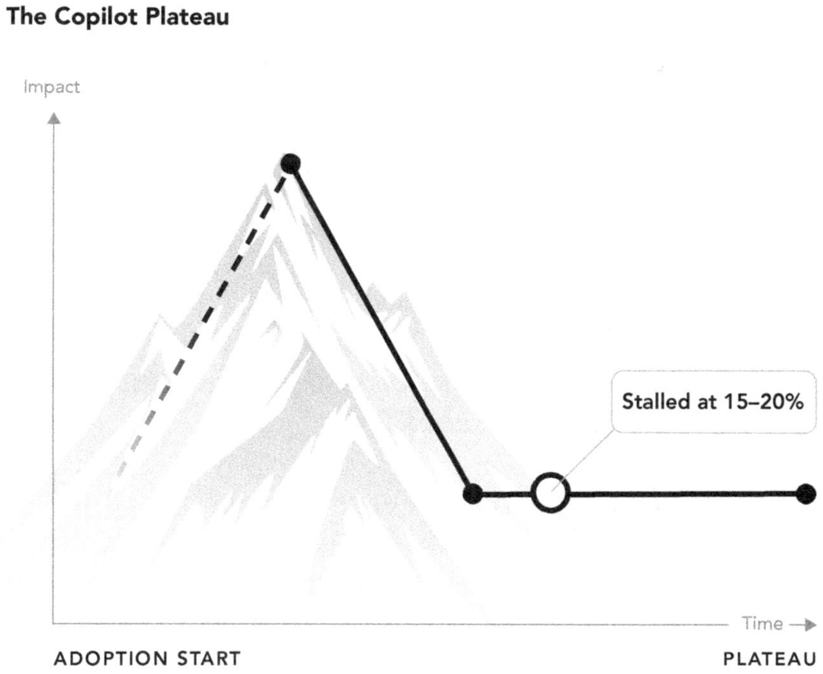

Figure 5.1 The Copilot Plateau. Enterprise AI adoption rises in the early weeks following rollout, then stalls at 15–20 percent of the eligible population when AI is deployed as a software rollout rather than introduced as a behavior change.

> *"Just my operation right now,"* she said, *"because if I go too far, the CIO will want to get involved. And I really don't want IT trying to take hold of it."*

Avery's instinct aligns with a pattern visible at the highest levels of organizational design. In 2025, Josh Bersin, who has spent decades studying HR leadership and organizational transformation, identified a growing number of companies in which the Chief People Officer, rather than the CIO, was leading enterprise AI adoption. The companies included Moderna, HubSpot, and even Microsoft. Each had moved the leadership responsibilities of AI transformation to the desks of their CPOs.[5] The most sophisticated companies in the world recognize AI adoption as a people problem, and the leaders best equipped to solve people problems are those who have been solving them throughout their careers.

As Vinay listened to Avery further describe her situation, he acknowledged the organizational complexity. Then he validated her instinct:

> *"We look at AI transformation in a more HR-centric way than we do in an IT kind of way. You, in your role in HR, should actually be leading AI adoption within the company. Because we think of AI as talent, not as technology."*

At OneDigital, the AI program runs through the people function. Our model centers on the AI Coworker. A Coworker is an AI given a specific job description, trained on specific knowledge, assigned a human supervisor who manages its development and performance, and made available to the people in the organization who need its capabilities. The Coworker has a name and a personality calibrated to the organization's culture. The Coworker also has a resume that documents its qualifications, its areas of expertise, and the kind of work it is equipped to help with. The Coworker moves through the same lifecycle the firm uses for any new hire, starting as an intern and graduating to apprentice work under a human manager. Promotion to full-time status follows once the Coworker has demonstrated reliable performance.

Every previous enterprise technology justified IT ownership because the technology did exactly what the user told it to do. The technology stayed in its lane, and IT was the right department to evaluate and deploy those tools and to keep them running for the next decade. The playbook worked for thirty years.

The accountant on the eighteenth floor of OneDigital does not type commands into a console when working with our AI finance Coworker. She has a conversation. When the Coworker's first response misses the mark, she pushes back, and the Coworker adjusts. Over time, the Coworker remembers her preferences. Producing work she would recognize as her own takes the same kind of development a senior leader would invest in any new hire.

The mechanics of building a Coworker program fill the next three chapters. The conceptual move at the heart of the second paradigm shift is from "We deployed an AI platform" to "We hired a team of specialists."

When companies give every employee Copilot or ChatGPT and call it enterprise AI, they are just giving everyone Excel. Excel handles budgeting in the hands of someone who knows the formulas. The accountant who has seen a hundred budgets go wrong brings judgment that a spreadsheet alone cannot match, and their institutional knowledge of which clients run aggressive forecasts and which board members react to a three-point miss travels with that accountant, building up over a career.

AI Coworkers let an organization hire the best accountant in the world and make that accountant available to every employee who needs help with budgeting.

The Charlotte-Denver problem disappears once both human consultants can work with the same AI Coworker. The training happens once. A senior practitioner at OneDigital, one who has handled ICHRA arrangements for a hundred manufacturing clients, walks the Coworker through their thinking. A human supervisor at the firm watches over the Coworker's development from there. Once onboarded, every consultant who needs the embedded expertise connects with the same AI Coworker, whether their own office sits in Atlanta, Phoenix, Boston, or any of OneDigital's 200 offices. Their work feeds back into the Coworker's knowledge base whenever a client question pushes into new territory.

The Coworker sharpens with every interaction it handles, and the institutional knowledge stays with the institution. On the call with Avery, Vinay explained why we built our Coworker program on a platform agnostic to any specific AI model. The platform could use models from Anthropic, OpenAI, Google, or other providers and switch among them as the competitive landscape shifts. OneDigital is not, and never will be, married to just one AI company.

> "*The other consideration to keep in mind,*" Vinay explained to Avery, "*is that when you use these platforms, you embed a lot of intelligence into them. And people worry about data lock-in. I've entered a lot of data into my CRM, and I can export it if I switch to a different CRM, as that data is valuable. Intelligence is like that, times ten.*"
>
> "*What you're doing is you're taking the know-how of how to run your business, and you're putting it into these AI systems. And they're getting developed and getting better, and they start to diverge and improve beyond the know-how of your own people. You're spending a lot of money retaining people because they have that know-how. But are you spending the same amount of effort to secure and retain the knowledge that you're giving all these AI systems?*"

Who owns the intelligence the firm is building? The intelligence inside an organization's AI Coworkers is an organizational asset. That intelligence is the accumulated expertise of the firm's best practitioners, encoded into systems every employee can access. The intelligence becomes vulnerable the moment it lives exclusively inside one vendor's platform, because vendors who control the platform also control the pricing schedule and the product roadmap.

OneDigital protects that intelligence aggressively, particularly the version encoded into our AI Coworkers.

AI agnosticism is the ability to move between AI model providers without losing the intelligence the firm has built. OneDigital would never issue a press release saying, "OneDigital is partnering with Anthropic" or "OneDigital is partnering with OpenAI." We use both. We will use whichever provider produces the best models for the work we need to do next quarter. The intelligence our Coworkers carry belongs to OneDigital, along with the expertise of our best practitioners encoded into systems available to every employee, regardless of which model the platform happens to run on. The platform-agnosticism point gets a much fuller treatment in Chapter 10.

For the first ten minutes of the call, Avery was guarded. The European parent company had told her "no" enough times that she was checking, sentence by sentence, whether Vinay's points would survive an executive review back in Europe. Halfway through the call, Avery was leaning forward in her frame. She finally had the language she needed to make her case to Europe. The framing she had been missing was AI transformation as a talent management problem belonging inside her HR remit.

> "*This makes me even more excited,*" she said. "*I think this is a huge opportunity. My thought is, if I can get HR moving at this level, the others will follow.*"

She described a new managing director who had recently arrived at the European parent company, with a strongly technology-forward posture. She described wanting to start with HR and prove the model, then use the evidence with European headquarters to expand into the other functions. In real time, Avery was planning an adoption strategy that started with the function she controlled and expanded based on demonstrated value.

"I'm so excited," Avery said at the end of the call. I believed her. The intonation matched the one in my own voice after my all-nighter. Avery had been holding a sense of urgency about AI for the better part of a year without a place to direct it. The call with Vinay gave her the direction.

The second paradigm shift moves the firm from individual collaboration to a connected enterprise capability that holds and grows institutional intelligence across the organization. In the language of the Workforce Intelligence Score, the shift carries the workforce into the upper two bands. Hundreds of workers in genuine collaboration with their AI move the workforce into the Performing range (0.55–0.82). Variable A approaches 1.00 only when AI Coworkers operate as genuine team members across the organization, putting the workforce inside the Leading band (0.82–1.00) and the fully blended state.

The mechanics of building that enterprise capability fill the next three chapters. The first walks through the work of writing a job description for an AI Coworker. The chapter after that covers the three-phase Coworker lifecycle. The hybrid workforce management structure that sustains the program over time is the third. The work runs through the management discipline that OneDigital's people leaders have practiced for years, with no technology background required.

So, Avery's question is how to get started. The answer begins with a job description.

6

Start with the Job Description

MIKE PICKS UP the phone and rattles cages until people move. My job at OneDigital involves the work that must happen after the conviction is in place. My name is Vinay Gidwaney, and I make sure that when people move, the path forward has been paved.

Before I joined the company, every feature of OneDigital's product was human-made. The advisors, consultants, and specialists who walked into a client's office and provided the guidance that justified our fees were human-operated at every level of the business. Today, the product is roughly 40 percent technology and 60 percent human, and that ratio will continue to shift.

The shift requires a product mindset, one that iterates based on instinct. This is a way of operating that is foreign to most organizations in our industry.

The methodology begins before any technology decision is made. Start with a job description. You decide who to hire and what you need them to do. You do the work the way every hiring manager in every organization has done it for decades: Writing a job description forces clarity.

The vocabulary an organization uses to describe its AI influences the deployment. If AI is described as a tool, a copilot, or a feature within enterprise software, its deployment will look like every other enterprise software rollout in the company's history. Six months in, the firm can expect to have a tool that sits within a workflow, is used by some, ignored by most, and generates a return well below the level of conviction that justified the spend.

At OneDigital, we use a different vocabulary for the purposes of our talent-centric deployment. We call our AI partners "Coworkers." An AI Coworker is a configured AI system that holds a defined role within a firm, performs work that other team members rely on, and reports to a named human supervisor.

The Coworker frame produces a different operating posture from day one. A named human owner hires and onboards the Coworker, then measures its performance by the quality of the work it produces and the time it returns to the human professionals around it. The Coworker sits inside a work center, the unit where information comes in and decisions go out (see Appendix C), configured to handle the parts where AI capabilities have overtaken human capabilities. The human professional retains the parts where intelligence is still irreducibly human. The six requirements that must be defined for any Coworker before implementation begins are shown in Figure 6.1.

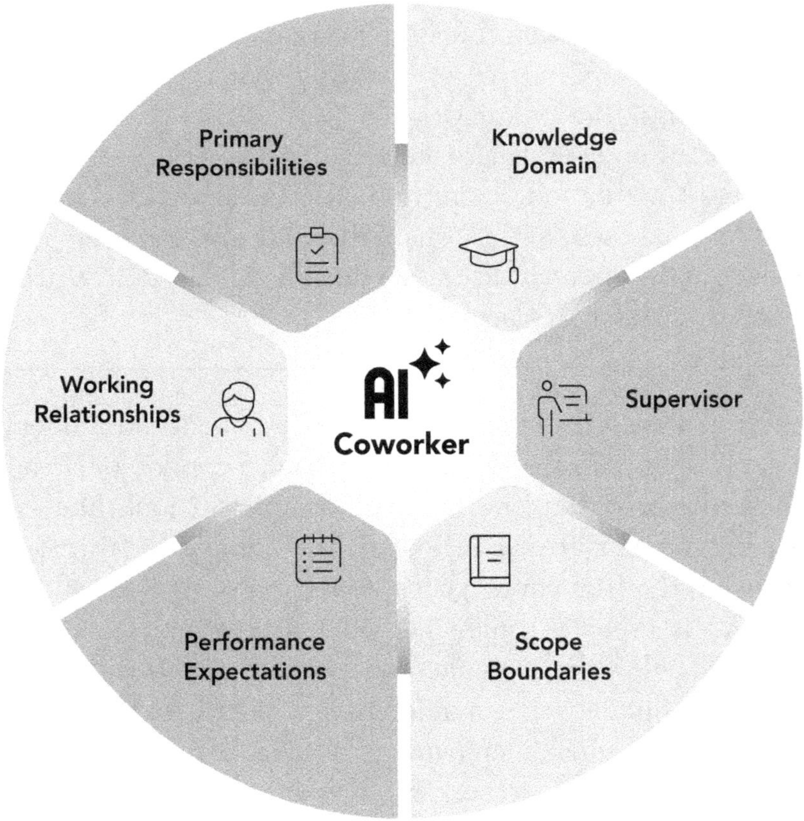

Figure 6.1 The six requirements of a Coworker job description—Knowledge Domain, Primary Responsibilities, Working Relationships, Performance Expectations, Scope Boundaries, and Supervisor—written before the technical implementation begins.

The phone call went out sometime in August of 2024. We were building what we internally called the 10x program, a working label for an effort that did not yet have a shape or a name. The premise was ambitious and vague in equal measure. We wanted to take the knowledge of our best practitioners and make it available to every employee in the company through AI. We had the conviction, though we had not yet worked out the method.

My call was to Shelley McLean.

Shelley is a veteran of the employee benefits business. Her title is National Growth Strategist, a role created to leverage her status as one of the most effective producers and consultants in the organization. One of her main responsibilities is training our 1,600-person employee benefits team across the country. She knows the business the way a surgeon knows anatomy and can translate her knowledge in ways that resonate with rooms full of people stressing about quarterly quotas.

I described the assignment to her: Consolidate your knowledge base into one place.

I told her to imagine she was training the best employee she had ever trained, and then to build that training into a system. Every document she would hand to a new hire, and every process she ran, had to be captured. Above all, I needed documentation on her approach to client conversations. That was central.

What I was asking her to build did not yet have a name. It would eventually become Ben, our first AI Coworker. In August of 2024, it was a slurry of an idea with no container. Shelley was the person I trusted to pour the foundation.

Her response to the assignment is why I tell her story first, before the frameworks, taxonomies, and scoring models that came later. Shelley got it right because she did not know enough about technology to get it wrong.

Where to Start

Shelley treated the assignment like hiring a person.

She did not ask for a technical specification or inquire about which large language model we planned to use. She sat down with the question every experienced hiring manager asks when they need to fill a role:

> **What do I need this person to do, and how do I need them to show up?**
>
> *"Ignorance was bliss,"* Shelley later said. *"We didn't know what we didn't know. And it proved to be a gift."*

What Shelley did instinctively, Ravin Jesuthasan has been arguing organizations must do deliberately. His framework for the skills-powered organization rests on deconstructing a job into its constituent tasks. For each task, he asks whether the intelligence required is best sourced from a person or from a partnership between a person and an AI. Sometimes the answer is that the task can be fully automated. The job description, in his formulation, describes work to be performed by the most capable intelligence available.[1]

Shelley arrived at the same place without the framework, because she asked the practitioner's version of his question. She thought about what an advisor needs to understand to show up the way she shows up after three decades in benefits consulting. She was mapping Ben's intelligence, though she did not yet have the language for it. The data pulls and plan comparisons that filled an advisor's workday were what most observers saw of Ben's work. The judgment Shelley had built over three decades about which client needed to hear what, and at what moment, was the part underneath. The job description Shelley wrote was for an AI that could carry the visible work, so the judgment, the part that was uniquely Shelley's, could reach more clients without thinning out.

The gift was that she bypassed the technology frame entirely. She never fell into the trap of writing a product requirements document, which is the document a technology-trained mind reaches for first. A product requirements document describes what a piece of software should do, in terms that a developer can build against. A job description describes a role and asks who you need on your team to be successful.

The person writing the job description must be a hiring manager, someone who has filled dozens of roles, knows where the persistent skill gaps lie inside the practice, and understands what a good day looks like for the team members this Coworker will serve. The work has to start from human need, not from the machine's capabilities.

Shelley knew her practice's skill gaps. Notably, public speaking was the skill most of her people feared. She knew the best consultants distinguished themselves by their ability to read the room, adjust their message for a CFO versus an HR director, and walk into a meeting prepared enough to make their client feel understood. Strong public speaking was the needle in the haystack, a rare combination of skills she sought whenever she posted a requisition.

So she designed a hire that would be the needle.

Shelley started with the output. "At the end of the day," she told me, "if I hire someone, they need to put me in a position to show up as the most effective, the most influential, and the most progressive consultant I can be." That output became the organizing principle of Ben's job description.

The Coworker's purpose was defined in terms of what the human could do with its help. A purpose stated as "analyze benefits data" would have produced an analysis engine. Shelley's purpose stated, "Help the consultant show up as the best version of themselves in front of a client." This statement produced a colleague.

Shelley's second decision was about knowledge boundaries. She selected the specific documents, data sources, and reference materials she would trust a new employee to use, and designed Ben to use those documents and no others. These were her authoritative sources.

She then taught Ben how to use those documents. She demonstrated how she would interpret them and explained what her standard was for her outputs. She was curating a curriculum, not loading a database.

Her third decision separated our approach from nearly every other enterprise AI deployment I have observed. Shelley told Ben to coach.

"When you give the consultant the data," she instructed Ben, "also tell them what to do with it and how to talk about it. If they are meeting with a CFO, give them the financial framing. If they are meeting with HR, give them the people framing. Identify the audience's personality and adjust the delivery accordingly. Give them the talk tracks."

Consultants partnered with Ben could walk into a meeting with preparation that would have taken hours to assemble manually. They would have advice on how to address each client or audience. And they would have pointers and key highlights to contribute to the conversation ahead.

A Coworker that operates the way Ben does delivers more than data. It supplies the data, the context, the delivery strategy, and the confidence to walk into a room knowing you are the most prepared person at the table. With Ben, Shelley was effectively designing several employees rolled into one. Ben is a researcher, an analyst, a communication coach, and a presentation specialist, applying all of those skills to the same knowledge base and all aimed at the same outcome. Such AI Coworkers make humans better at the work that requires a human.

What Shelley did instinctively, we later codified into a set of frameworks that have guided every Coworker deployment since. The frameworks emerged from observing what worked and what did not across eighteen Coworker hires, and they prevent the most common mistake in enterprise AI: choosing the wrong problem to solve first.

The first framework is a taxonomy of work. Before writing a job description, you need to know what job you are hiring for. This requires more consideration than simply asking, "Can AI perform this task, yes or no?"

The right approach has three considerations:

1. Can AI perform the work well enough to be trusted?
2. Will the reallocation of human time create real value?
3. Does that value justify the required investment?

When going through these considerations, our experience produced four categories that have proven reliable as a sorting mechanism: Eliminate, Redesign, Retain, and Create.

Eliminate: High-volume, rule-based tasks with clear right answers. Formatting reports, answering frequently asked first-tier questions, populating templates, generating draft summaries, and normalizing data across carrier formats. The AI performs the work end-to-end. The human is removed from the loop because the human's time is more valuable than the task demands. These workflows are satisfying to automate, but they are rarely where the greatest value lies, because the tasks themselves are rarely where the greatest time burden lies.

Redesign: The richest of the four categories. In a Redesign workflow, the AI produces analyses, drafts, and research while the human directs, reviews, and makes key decisions. The human's role does not shrink, but shifts to areas of greater significance to the business. The benefits consultant who used to spend four hours assembling benchmarking data before a renewal meeting now spends twenty minutes reviewing the data Ben assembled. The time saved can be put toward relationship-building actions that Ben cannot (or should not) execute. Redesign is our recommended starting point because the results are immediate, visible, and felt by the frontline workers. Shelley's design for Ben was a Redesign from the start, before we had a name for the category.

Retain: Covers tasks where AI adds little or where the human element is itself the value. The conversation with a sixty-year-old widow about her retirement plan. The difficult phone call when an employee learns their claim has been denied and needs someone who will listen. The presentation to a board of directors, where trust is earned by the presence and judgment of a person with years of credibility. Identifying what to retain matters as much as identifying what to redesign. This boundary protects the human contribution from being eroded by enthusiasm for the technology.

Create: Capabilities that did not exist before AI made them possible. Predictive analytics on health claims trends across a client portfolio. Real-time compliance monitoring that catches errors before they reach a regulatory body. Proactive risk identification that alerts an advisor to a client's emerging exposure before the client knows to ask. Create is the most exciting category. It is also the worst place to start an AI Coworker program. Until your organization has a baseline to measure against, an existing workflow to improve upon, and an established user group for a Create task, focus on Redesign and Retain.

Eliminate	Redesign	Retain	Create
High-volume, rule-based work with clear right answers. AI handles end-to-end; humans review by exception.	AI drafts, analyzes, and proposes; humans direct, review, and decide. The richest category and the right place to start.	Work where the human element is the value. AI adds little. Conversations of judgment, trust, and moral weight.	Capabilities that did not exist before AI. The most exciting category and the worst place to start a Coworker program.

When a leadership team sits down to identify its first Coworker, knowing that Redesign workflows produce the best combination of visible impact, adoption quality, and manageable risk gives them focus, where an open field of possibilities tends to produce paralysis. Within the Redesign category, strong first-deployment candidates share a set of characteristics:

- The work happens often (daily, weekly, or with every client engagement), so the Coworker gets used to it and builds a working relationship.
- The expertise required is documented in policies, data, and established practices, rather than residing solely in the heads of veterans.
- A domain expert can review the output and tell whether it is correct.
- The human review step can be completed quickly enough that the time savings do not disappear into the act of reviewing.
- The people doing the work feel the time burden, so adoption pulls rather than pushes.

Shelley's benefits consulting workflow checked every one of those boxes. The work happened daily. The knowledge base was documented across carrier relationships and regulatory frameworks. The quality was verifiable against industry standards. The time burden was real and felt by every consultant on the team. An experienced advisor could review and refine Ben's output in minutes rather than hours. Ben was a perfect candidate for deployment.

The organizations that get their first deployment right make every subsequent deployment faster. During the first hire, they are building muscle memory for Coworker management. They will use this muscle again during the subsequent deployments.

Organizations that get the first deployment wrong spend the following year managing the skepticism that a failed first impression produces. Organizational doubt about AI capability, once established through a deployment that overpromised and underdelivered, is difficult to overcome. The second deployment starts in a hole that the first one dug. The patience required to identify the right problem compounds into returns that impatient organizations never recover.

Writing the Job Description

So, how did Shelley write the job description?

Ben's job description has six elements. Each one forces a decision that most technology deployments never require, and each one produces a management discipline that pays returns long after the initial build is complete.

The First Requirement: The Knowledge Domain

What must your AI Coworker know in order to do its job?

Shelley's instinct proved most valuable in Ben's case. She selected the specific documents, data sources, regulatory and market references, and organizational materials she considered authoritative. A benefits Coworker at OneDigital must know the firm's carrier relationships and pricing dynamics across different market segments. It must also know the specific benefit designs that have performed well for clients of different sizes and industries. The same goes for regulatory requirements in the relevant markets, the language employee benefits advisors use with clients, and the ways complex benefit decisions get explained to HR directors who are not insurance specialists.

The knowledge domain is not just a one-and-done consideration. It makes the Coworker's continuing education plan concrete. When the market changes, when regulations shift, and when the firm adds new carrier relationships, the Coworker's knowledge needs to be updated. This means that the Supervisor managing that update needs to know what to update and why.

The Second Requirement: Primary Responsibilities

Primary responsibilities sit at the heart of the job description. Three to five core functions, stated specifically, are tied to outcomes the business cares about. A software specification would say the system assists with research. A job description says the Coworker prepares client situation summaries ahead of advisory meetings, identifying key renewal risk factors, relevant benchmark comparisons, and the strategic questions the advisor should be prepared to address.

The more specific the responsibilities are, the better. No "and anything else the Supervisor asks for" clauses. Specificity serves two management functions: It sets clear expectations for the people who will work alongside the Coworker and provides the basis for performance evaluation. These are the responsibilities that the Supervisor will assess.

The Third Requirement: Working Relationships

Who does this Coworker serve? Who interacts with it daily?

Working relationships must be named explicitly. Documenting these relationships produces management discipline. With the relationships written down, the Supervisor knows exactly which human coworker's daily practice the AI Coworker is integrated into, and can monitor the quality of those relationships over time.

The Fourth Requirement: Performance Expectations

Performance expectations must be defined and mapped to a timeline.

What does success look like at 30 days, at 90 days, and at one year? Who is responsible for the evaluations?

These questions separate Coworkers that improve over time from those that plateau. If success cannot be defined within these parameters, then the team is not ready for deployment. In this case, best to go back to square one and reconsider what a good Redesign role might be for the Coworker.

The Fifth Requirement: Scope Boundaries

Scope boundaries belong in the job description and must be stated explicitly. AI Coworkers will deliver better outputs when they know what *not* to do. This saves time, energy, and tokens (which equate to money).

Setting scope boundaries governs the Coworker, preventing it from operating outside its competence. It also sets accurate expectations for users, so that a first interaction falls within the Coworker's capabilities. A Coworker that disappoints on the first interaction, no matter the reason, has lost credibility that is expensive to rebuild.

The Sixth Requirement: The Supervisor

Every Coworker must have a named human Supervisor before the build begins. This is nonnegotiable. The Supervisor role is not a position to be filled after deployment. It is a precondition of deployment.

The Supervisor curates the Coworker's intelligence, monitors its performance, updates its knowledge base as the market shifts, reviews user feedback, and decides what to improve. The Supervisor is the management infrastructure that allows the Coworker to develop beyond its initial capabilities. Without that infrastructure, the Coworker plateaus at whatever quality it achieves on day one.

A Coworker without a Supervisor is like a new employee without a manager. The work might be acceptable in the first month, but growth stops there. Gaps in the Coworker's knowledge go unidentified, edge cases go unaddressed, and feedback that would improve it never gets collected.

How do you choose a Supervisor? The Supervisor should be the person in the organization whose work best exemplifies what the Coworker is designed to deliver. This could be the best sales producer, the most respected consultant, or the sharpest analyst on the team. Find these people and enable them to amplify their impact through a Coworker. Take someone who can currently influence fifty clients through their personal practice, and empower them to reach 300, 500, 1,500 people.

Framing this correctly will alleviate your human workers' fears. In Shelley's case, she is extending her reach rather than training her replacement. The Coworker brings her expertise, standards, and approach to client situations to every benefits consultant in the company. Shelley's value has *increased* because Ben's value is a function of Shelley's knowledge. With her behind it, acting as its Supervisor, Ben becomes the institutional embodiment of three decades of consulting excellence. Without her, Ben is just a specially curated chatbot.

When I talk to prospective Supervisors, I frame the work this way. First, you become great at your craft. Then you teach it. Teaching is the highest form of professional contribution, and the AI Coworker is the medium that enables you to teach at an unprecedented scale. By supervising a Coworker, your knowledge and standards are available to anyone in the organization who needs them, at any time, day or night, without you needing to be in the room.

The question of incentive is real, and we are studying it formally with economists from MIT and Harvard Business School. The right models for rewarding Supervisors for their contributions remain an open question, whether public attribution, compensation adjustments, career advancement, or some combination we have not yet identified. The Supervisor's willingness to invest in the Coworker depends, over time, on whether the organization visibly values that investment.

For now, the motivation we have observed in our early Supervisors has been intrinsic. They watch consultants who were struggling with a particular skill suddenly perform at a higher level because their AI Coworker coached them through it. They hear from clients who received better, deeper, more timely analysis because the Coworker freed their advisors from hours of manual preparation. They see their own expertise making an impact in a way that is both visible and measurable, a form of professional validation that most experienced practitioners have never received.

Shelley is the model. She reviews Ben's performance data monthly and updates his knowledge base as the business evolves. These updates consist of new training materials, carrier information, and consulting approaches. She does this work with the broader team in mind. She also runs a national training series called Breaking Benefit Barriers, and whenever she creates new content for it, she updates Ben at the same time. She trains the human team and the AI Coworker in parallel, which keeps the organization's knowledge synchronized rather than fragmented across separate channels.

The Supervisor's monthly investment in keeping the Coworker's intelligence current with the organization's requirements is what drives year-over-year improvements in the WI Score.

Specialist Coworkers

As Ben matured and proved the model, we applied the same process to build specialists across every major practice area. One of the earliest and most consequential design decisions in the program was to build many specialized Coworkers rather than one general-purpose AI available to the entire organization.

The instinct most organizations follow, because it is the instinct the software framework produces, is to deploy a single AI platform with broad capability across the company: one tool, one training program, one dashboard, and one vendor relationship. The simplicity is appealing. The economics look better on a spreadsheet. The IT and procurement teams prefer it. The problem is that it does not work at the depth the talent model demands. It offers broad availability and modest usage, but fails to generate outputs credible enough to change user behavior.

Take the same question asked of a generic AI and of Ben. A consultant types a prompt: "I have a 200-life manufacturing employer with 68 percent participation in the health plan, a $2,500-deductible Blue Cross Blue Shield plan, and a 12 percent trend increase in premiums. What benchmarking data should I bring to the renewal, and what alternatives should I consider?"

The generic AI produces a broadly correct, shallow response. It references general benchmarking concepts, noting that deductibles vary by industry, and suggests some standard cost-containment strategies. The output lacks specific manufacturing benchmarks, a participation rate analysis relative to the industry median, and is not formatted in OneDigital's standard style. The consultant reads it and decides it is marginally more helpful than what they already knew.

Ben produces a structured analysis with current manufacturing sector benchmarks, flags the 68 percent participation rate as below the 74 percent industry median, models three alternative scenarios with cost projections, and formats the output as an executive summary in OneDigital's standard style. The consultant reviews, makes two adjustments based on the relationship context that Ben lacks, and walks into the meeting with confidence.

The underlying AI model may be the same, but the difference is specialization. The knowledge base, the instructions, and the domain-specific training tell the AI what "good" looks like for the people it serves. Specialization changes what sits in the context window, how the AI interprets the question, and what quality means for the domain the Coworker operates within.

The Coworker portfolio at OneDigital is a roster of specialists, each with a specific domain, a named Supervisor, and a defined knowledge base. The supervisors of these Coworkers, the people whose expertise Ben and his colleagues now carry to every consultant in the firm, have taken on a dimension of their professional contribution that did not exist when they were hired. Their reach is roughly an order of magnitude beyond what their personal practice alone could produce.

Coworker	Domain	Supervisor(s)
Ben	Employee benefits	Shelley McLean
Dex	Sales intelligence and prospect analysis	Emily Knott, Dean Ray
Nina	Executive benefits and nonqualified deferred compensation	Nick Gibbings
Jackie	Form 5500 analysis for the retirement practice	Allie Rivera
Avery	Property and Casualty property research	Greg Jones, Dallas Arnaudo
Quinn	Property and Casualty quote normalization	Scott P'Pool, Dallas Arnaudo
Amy	Property and Casualty risk assessment	(Practice rotation)
Odysseus	M&A due diligence	Mark Nasca
Charity	Not-for-profit vertical	Matt O'Neill
Ace	Cross-practice generalist for tasks without deep domain expertise	(Cross-practice)

The pattern copies how humans already operate. People in any organization route their hard questions to the colleague with the deepest expertise in the relevant domain, and they are skeptical of generalists who claim coverage across the board. A Coworker portfolio that mirrors that instinct (a roster of named specialists in place of a single, all-purpose assistant) is more approachable.

With a specialist approach, working relationships between humans and AI Coworkers develop, driving deeper value over time. Deployments that try to install a single omniscient AI for the whole company underperform because the relationship structure doesn't reflect the most trusting collaborations.

Each Coworker in the portfolio began the way Ben did. Someone identified a need, wrote a job description, and assigned a Supervisor. An iterative process of building, testing, and refining followed. That process, repeated across practices and the country, turned Shelley's AI Coworker experiment into a whole portfolio.

The primary attribute that made Shelley's work possible was a product mindset. A product mindset is the willingness to start before you feel ready, ship before it is perfect, and iterate based on what you learn. Ben is on his nineteenth iteration because Shelley has been iterating continuously since August of 2024. She has added instructions, refined knowledge, adjusted the communication style, expanded the scope, and created new use case templates based on what she discovered in the field. Today, Ben is measurably better than he was six months ago, and six months from now, Ben will be better still.

So, with the job description written and the Supervisor named, what's the next step? You make the hire, of course! Except you're not going to hire a full-time AI Coworker right off the bat. Instead, the Coworker's lifecycle will start as any new hire's does: with an internship.

7

Hiring Ben: The Three-Phase Lifecycle

After writing the job description, most organizations make the same mistake: They treat the hiring process as a switch flip. They configure the platform, grant access, announce it, and instruct people to use the Coworker. Then, even with a fully fleshed-out job description and one-year improvement plan, the Coworker's adoption plateaus after a few months. Most users are so frustrated with the initial release that they don't even bother to provide feedback.

This is how even a well-designed job description can fail on deployment.

The organizations that get deployment right do something else: They develop the Coworker the way they develop any new employee. They use phases, gates, constant supervision, and actionable feedback.

Any new colleague, human or otherwise, does not arrive fully formed. It grows into the role through the quality of the management it receives.

At OneDigital, our AI Coworker hiring process has three phases: Internship, Apprenticeship, and Full-Time. The **Internship** is the discovery phase, where the Coworker is stress-tested against real examples of the work and where the knowledge base is curated, refined, and corrected in an iterative loop. The **Apprenticeship** is the development phase, where the Coworker is deployed to a carefully selected subset of users who serve as mentors. The mentors provide feedback that drives the next round of improvements. **Full-Time** availability is when a Coworker enters a continuous performance cycle, running quarterly reviews like any other team member and evolving as the business does. Each phase has its own discipline, its own standard for progression, and its own failure modes.

None of this happens in a vacuum. While the Coworker is in development, the humans who will work with it are trained on how to collaborate with it. The Intern Coworker's curriculum runs in parallel with that of the eventual mentors. One without the other inevitably produces one of two outcomes: an untrained Coworker no one trusts, or a Coworker no one uses because the team was not taught how. Both modes of failure are common and preventable.

Phase One: Internship

The Internship phase begins the moment the initial build is complete. This means the Coworker has a knowledge base, a set of instructions, access to a defined pool of reference materials, and a personality calibrated to the practice it serves. On paper, it is ready to work. In practice, it is a rookie with a resume written by an optimist.

Robin Singhvi, who runs our AI program, has the cleanest way of framing this phase for the small cohort of users brought in to test the Coworker. The Supervisor already knows the Coworker is a rookie. The Cohort needs to hear it explicitly. As Robin explains:

> *"If a Coworker is an intern, that means that means it will make mistakes. The Coworker in front of them is a rough draft, deliberately so, and their job is to stress-test the accuracy and comprehensiveness of its knowledge base. We want to ensure our instructions are coherent and lead to consistently good answers. The Internship is the quality-assurance cycle that prevents the launch from failing."*

The rollout during the Internship is deliberately narrow. We do not expose a new Coworker to all 6,000 employees at once. We run a pipeline, with Coworkers at different stages of maturity, each exposed to the subset of people who can produce useful feedback for that stage.

Organizations that skip this step in the interest of speed pay for the shortcut with a first impression from which it is hard to fully recover. A Coworker that disappoints twenty users in week one creates a perception among those users that will take months to reverse, regardless of how good the Coworker becomes later.

During the Internship, there is an iterative loop among the Supervisor, the user cohort, and the AI team. A Coworker never progresses from Intern to Apprentice without going through multiple iteration cycles. Each cycle produces refinements to the knowledge base and to the instructions that govern how the Coworker uses it. Does it pull from the open web, or only from the knowledge base we provided? Is it weighing recent documents the way we want it to? Does the output match the format our consultants expect? Each of those questions gets worked through iteration, and each iteration produces a slightly sharper version of the Coworker.

The Internship phase takes time. Shelley ran this process for Ben for the better part of a year, from August 2024 through the spring of 2025. She and Robin were, in her words, "together like every day with the evolution of Ben." The cadence was a daily refinement. Shelley would surface a case where the Coworker made an error. Robin would trace the failure to a gap in the knowledge base or an instruction that needed rewriting, and enter the fix. The next day, another test would expose another weakness, and the cycle would repeat. They did this for eight months. That is what Internship-grade iteration looks like when it is done properly, and why I caution organizations to give themselves time.

Somewhere in that stretch of months, Shelley watched Ben produce an output that made her pause. She had been stress-testing him on a real client scenario, the kind she would have spent an afternoon preparing for in the past. The output came back accurate, structured in the format her team used, with benchmarking context she had not explicitly asked for and talk tracks calibrated to the client-side decision-maker. She sat back at her desk. She had trained many new hires over her career, but she had never seen one produce work so close to her standard in such a short amount of time.

That was the moment Ben, the AI Coworker, became real to her, and the moment the Coworker program became real inside OneDigital. Shelley, the practitioner who had spent three decades earning the right to be skeptical, believed in Ben before Mike, me, or any of the executives who had approved the budget.

Such moments arise when the knowledge base reaches a threshold of depth, and the practitioner's standards find a partner capable of meeting them. Until then, the Coworker remains a prototype whose development is still uncertain. The Internship exists to identify when that moment has arrived.

By the time the broader cohort meets the Coworker, the Coworker already knows the practice. The outputs meet the team's standards, meaning the first interaction can confirm what was promised, and the working relationship can accelerate from there. The collaborative use of AI begins.

Phase Two: Apprenticeship

When the Coworker has cleared the Internship, meaning the knowledge base is reliable enough and the instructions coherent enough for the Supervisor to sign off, it moves into the Apprenticeship.

Every phase of the lifecycle pairs the Supervisor with a cohort, and the cohort widens as the Coworker matures. The Internship cohort is small, drawn from the people closest to the work and best positioned to surface gaps. Apprenticeship widens the cohort, bringing the Coworker into contact with a larger slice of the practice and generating feedback that shapes the final capability.

A well-run Apprenticeship has features that distinguish it from a standard software pilot.

Genuine stakes come first. Feedback from a controlled test environment tells you only how a Coworker performs in a controlled test environment, while feedback from daily practice tells you how it performs in the space where it will live. The work during the Apprenticeship phase is the practice's actual work: real clients, real deadlines, and real consequences for quality.

Next, the feedback loop must have teeth. Users mark outputs with a thumbs-up or thumbs-down, send notes when an output falls short, and flag cases where a Coworker hallucinated or misread context. The Supervisor synthesizes that feedback weekly and works with Robin's team to address the systematic gaps it surfaces. Organizations that collect feedback during pilots and then fail to act on it train their users to stop giving feedback. The Apprenticeship phase builds the feedback relationship to sustain the Coworker's development for years after it reaches full availability.

The resume also gets its first substantive update. The Coworker arrived at the Internship with a resume already drafted, which informed the KPIs and the job description, and served as the north star for the initial build. The Apprenticeship earns the resume its first revision based on real performance. This ensures that the knowledge domain sharpens as gaps are filled and edge cases are cataloged. Situations where the Coworker performs well get documented alongside those that still require human oversight, and the integrations that have proven reliable are formalized for the broader team.

The job description and KPIs evolve in lockstep with the resume. The updated package serves as onboarding material for colleagues who will work with the Coworker once it is fully deployed. It continues to evolve through subsequent phases as feedback accumulates and capabilities mature. A Coworker with a clear and current resume is a Coworker the team can engage with under accurate expectations.

One dynamic we did not anticipate during the Apprenticeship turned out to be among the most powerful drivers of adoption at scale. The users in the pilot felt they were helping train Ben, and that participation produced a form of investment that a polished launch could never have created. Shelley told me that the team members who gave thumbs-up and thumbs-down were the same people who eventually evangelized Ben to their colleagues. They had a stake in him. They had shaped him. Asking them to help, instead of presenting them with a finished product, made them partners in the development.

This is why, in my experience, compressing the Apprenticeship phase is the most expensive shortcut an organization can take. The pressure to compress is real. The CFO wants to see results. The practice leader wants the Coworker rolled out. The AI team has a roadmap with other builds waiting behind this one.

The arithmetic runs the other way.

A Coworker released before the Apprenticeship is complete is one whose gaps will be visible to users who cannot unsee them. In the fast-moving world of AI, the last thing a company can afford to be doing is recovering from a bad first impression. The four to eight weeks you cut from the Apprenticeship become six months spent rebuilding the team's willingness to engage.

Not every Coworker makes it through.

"I've fired so many Coworkers by now," Robin joked to our editorial team, "that when AI truly becomes sentient, I'll be first on their list."

We treat Coworker development with the same honesty we treat human development. Some hires do not work out, just as some ideas that sounded promising in a meeting fail to survive contact with the work. When that becomes clear, the humane response is to vocalize it, end it, and move on. It's better than letting the Coworker drift into perpetual mediocrity that wastes everyone's time.

The question at every stage is whether the Coworker executes the job description well enough to justify continued investment. The Supervisor evaluates the quality of the outputs against practice standards and the net time savings the Coworker produces for the cohort. Based on the analysis, the Coworker either progresses to the next phase or holds in place with a remediation plan. The third option, sunset, is reserved for Coworkers whose remediation has not produced results. There is no fourth option.

A Coworker allowed to linger in ambiguity consumes the Supervisor's attention and the AI team's bandwidth, eroding the organization's credibility without producing value. Allowing the drift to happen is itself a form of governance failure, and one we have worked hard to prevent.

Sunsets rarely come from a technical failure. The most common cause is that the Coworker was solving the wrong problem to begin with. An idea that seemed compelling in a brainstorm turned out to address a task already well-served by an existing tool, or a task that did not have enough volume to justify the infrastructure, or a task where the human element was the value and the analytical layer was not the bottleneck. When that becomes clear, the right response is to document what worked, document what failed, thank the Supervisor publicly, and redirect the investment to the next build.

The second most common reason for sunsetting an AI Coworker is a Supervisor who could not or would not do the work. We have had cases where a senior leader was assigned the role by title rather than by motivation, and the Coworker's knowledge base went weeks without an update. Feedback from the cohort went unreviewed, and adoption among the team declined as the Coworker fell further behind in development.

A disengaged Supervisor does more damage than no Supervisor at all. What happens is that the supervising role's existence creates an illusion of management, while the absence of supervising work erodes both the Coworker's capability and the team's trust. When we see that pattern, we have learned to have a candid conversation as soon as possible. Either recruit a different Supervisor or sunset the AI Coworker and return the capacity to the team.

Phase Three: Full-Time

When a Coworker completes the Apprenticeship with the Supervisor's sign-off, it graduates to Full-Time. This means full availability to everyone in the practice it was built to serve. It is integrated into human onboarding, training, and the team's daily rhythm.

Graduation to Full-Time is where the compounding dynamic operates at scale. The wider user base produces more feedback, which supports continued development. This ongoing improvement encourages more users to collaborate and provide feedback.

Shelley has described Ben's first six months at Full-Time as the period when the curve went from linear to accelerating. In that short time, the Coworker that took eight months to build reached a level of capability that would have taken three years to achieve without the compounding feedback from the wider team.

The Supervisor's role at Full-Time shifts from building to managing. Shelley runs two cadences. The first is a monthly feedback review, where she sits down with the thumbs-up and thumbs-down data and the open ticket queue to identify what needs to be fixed or refined. Then there is a deeper, quarterly back-room review, where she looks at Ben's entire performance profile. Which use cases have the highest satisfaction, and which ones have the most drop-off? Where is Ben being used in ways the team had not predicted, and should those patterns be formalized? Where is the scope insufficient, and where does the redirection language need sharpening?

The quarterly review produces a formal performance assessment, and that assessment follows the same process as every serious human performance review. What was this Coworker hired to do? How well is it performing? Where are the gaps? What is the development plan for the next 90 days?

The output Shelley produces is an updated resume that communicates to the team what Ben can do better than he could three months ago. The updated resume also signals to the team that Ben is developing professionally alongside them.

When the quarterly review surfaces problems, the remediation path is defined. Metrics below the threshold for one cycle trigger a root cause analysis and a thirty-day reevaluation. Sustained adoption decline or persistent accuracy issues bring the Coworker back to Apprentice status, where it operates under restricted use while the gaps are addressed. Continued failure ends in a sunset.

Documenting and enforcing those paths is the discipline that keeps Full-Time status meaningful. A Coworker at Full-Time is a Coworker that the organization has agreed is capable of producing value at the standard of the practice. The willingness to demote a Coworker when the work no longer meets that standard is what gives the Full-Time label its meaning.

Ongoing Supervisor Education

An AI Coworker is a colleague whose quality is a function of the management it receives. Without an engaged Supervisor, the Coworker plateaus at whatever level it reached on the day it graduated. With an engaged Supervisor, the quality curve continues to rise.

As mentioned in the previous chapter, Shelley runs a national training series called Breaking Benefit Barriers, delivered to the employee benefits team every three weeks. She uses the series to teach about current industry dynamics, emerging regulatory issues, new carrier programs, and the tactical adjustments her team should make to client conversations in response. Every time she creates a new training module for the 1,600 consultants on the benefits team, she updates Ben's knowledge base in parallel. In her words, she is training Ben as she is training the entire team. The two curricula move in lockstep.

The effect of that parallel evolution over twelve months is a Coworker who looks qualitatively different from the one who graduated to Full-Time a year earlier. In early 2025, Ben needed to be told which sources to draw from. Users had to begin each prompt with an explicit instruction to rely only on reputable documents, ask for talk tracks instead of expecting them by default, and specify audience-specific framing depending on whether the client-side interlocutor was a CFO or an HR director. Each of those instructions had to be in every prompt, which is why Shelley taught the team a four-question prompting template in the early months. "Ben, I need you to . . . Using these sources . . . Structured in this format . . . Written for this audience . . ." Consistent, repeatable, and unnecessarily tedious.

A year later, none of those instructions are needed. Ben defaults to reputable sources because the Supervisor's feedback taught him which sources to trust. Talk tracks now come unprompted because the team consistently asked for them, and the pattern was formalized into his instructions. The audience-specific framing also became standard operating procedure, with Ben adjusting his delivery based on the client-side personality without explicit prompting.

The users have also evolved. The four-question template is no longer needed. They talk to Ben the way they would talk to a colleague they have worked with for a year. The scaffolding has been internalized by both parties, and the collaboration has become faster and more natural as a result.

That is what continuing education looks like when the Supervisor takes it seriously. Neither the Coworker nor the team plateaus. They develop together, with each step in the Coworker's evolution matched by a corresponding step in the team's fluency.

This is the compounding advantage that distinguishes organizations that get the first deployment right. The first Coworker builds the institutional muscle for managing Coworkers. The Supervisor learns what the role requires, the team learns what working alongside a developing colleague looks like, and the AI team learns what production-quality iteration looks like in the specific context of the practice. By the time the second Coworker enters the Internship phase, the entire organization is operating with a set of capabilities that the first Coworker's Supervisor had to build from scratch. The third Coworker, the fourth, and the rest enter at increasing speed, with fewer corrections during Apprenticeship and more consistent outcomes at Full-Time.

What does adoption look like when it exceeds compliance and becomes human-AI collaboration?

Shelley's inbox lit up recently when Ben was down for a few minutes. The outage did not affect any deadlines. Consultants across the country noticed "he was not there" and reached out to tell her, "Ben is off today." "Is Ben okay?" Shelley took screenshots and sent them to Robin and me.

That is what adoption looks like: a team that notices their Coworker is absent, the way they would notice a colleague being out sick, and reaches out to the Supervisor the way they would reach out to a manager. The relationship is real. The AI Coworker has become a member of the team.

The numbers underneath that behavior are worth sharing for context. OneDigital introduced its updated and expanded Coworker platform at our national Summit in early March 2026. Twenty people were on the new platform at launch. Six weeks later, the number exceeded 2,800, with 1,500 weekly active users among a workforce of 6,000.

Ben is part of every onboarding program and every monthly training Shelley runs across the country. Consultants refer to Ben by name at water-cooler moments. People ask, "What did Ben say?" the way they would ask what a trusted senior colleague said.

The Coworker does the work it was built to do, the Supervisor's monthly investment keeps it sharp, and the team has folded the relationship into their operations. Also, anthropomorphizing is an intentional design choice (more on that in a later chapter). We believe it has produced the working relationship that the Coworker model was built to enable.

Even with all of Ben's success, a single Coworker does not make an organization capable of AI-driven transformation at scale. Ben proved the model and taught the institution what Coworker management requires. Scaling from one practice to the rest of the firm, and from one Supervisor to a system of them managing dozens of Coworkers, requires structures, roles, a training architecture, and a leadership posture that no single deployment can produce on its own.

Turning Ben into a portfolio, and turning that portfolio into a genuine hybrid workforce, is the work that comes next.

8

Building the Hybrid Workforce

On a Saturday morning in March of 2026, I was about to email Adam with a budget request for ten new Enterprise Product Manager roles. Each EPM at OneDigital is the technical partner who works alongside a Coworker Supervisor, translating domain knowledge into platform configuration, prompt engineering, integrations, and analytics. If the Supervisor is Batman, then the EPM is Lucius Fox.

As the Coworker portfolio grew across the firm, the EPM team became the bottleneck. Each new Coworker added configuration work, analytics dashboards, integration tasks, and office hours. The math seemed simple. Add ten EPMs at roughly $200,000 each, fully loaded, and you have increased the organization's capacity to grow its workforce intelligence.

My letter to Adam was drafted and ready to send, but then Mike and I had a conversation that changed my mind.

Within days, I sent Adam a different letter. It opens this way:

> *"I was about to send you an email with the budget to expand the EPM team. The ask was for ten additional roles and other items, totaling around $2 million. But, after noodling on this more and having a good conversation with Mike this weekend, I believe we are thinking about this the wrong way."*

The argument in the letter rested on a single observation. With AI, the barrier to building technology has collapsed. The specialized engineering knowledge that once made application development the domain of a centralized product or technology team is now, for a growing class of applications, accessible to anyone with domain expertise, the right infrastructure, and training to use AI development tools. An application that two years ago would have required a six-figure engineering budget and months of development time can now be built by a domain expert in days.

Expanding the central team is the wrong response to that change. It treats technology development as a specialized practice, even though its defining feature is accessibility to non-specialists. Expanding the EPM team would double down on centralization, even as the ability to efficiently decentralize became possible.

The alternative proposed in the letter was a Fellowship. We would select ten people from across the business, bring them to Atlanta for three days of intensive training, and return them to their practices ready to build the tools their teams need. The names in the letter were real people who had already demonstrated the product instinct and domain depth that the program would encourage. These individuals just needed infrastructure and formal support to become builders.

The idea for the Fellowship program came from a specific insight that Mike and I had on our call: When building is cheap and fast, the competitive advantage shifts to the organization that best knows what to build. That capability belongs to the business side rather than the technology side. And the organizations best at knowing what to build are those whose builders are embedded in the practices they build for.

Centralization is an artifact of an old constraint. The instinct to hire new EPMs was old muscle memory, inconsiderate of present AI capabilities. Today, even an organization as large as OneDigital is more than capable of distributing the necessary skill sets to existing workers and supporting their expanded responsibilities through a shared infrastructure. We just had to design the program and its support infrastructure.

Adam approved the redirect.

The original Fellowship concept evolved as we ran it. Two complementary programs also emerged for "Fellows" and "Builders." Fellows took the role of super users and adoption champions, pushing the boundaries of how AI Coworkers are used in their practice and pulling colleagues forward. Builders took the technical path, instructing AI to write the code that turns ideas into shipped tools. Both roles are essential to the architecture in operation at OneDigital today.

But neither role is as essential as the mental reset required of all leaders and participants involved in our AI transformation . . .

One more note before I get into the architecture of OneDigital's hybrid workforce.

The letter I sent Adam emerged from a posture Mike and I had been embracing for months, one I have started calling "Founder Mode" after the framing Paul Graham popularized in his blog in 2024.[1] Graham's essay drew on a talk by Brian Chesky, in which he described how the conventional advice to "hire good people and give them room to do their jobs" had nearly broken Airbnb during its scale-up. Chesky concluded that a more direct, hands-on engagement with the substance of the company's work was the better path forward for its leaders. Graham's extrapolation was to give the posture a name and to argue that the conventional wisdom about how to run a large company was, for many companies, the source of their stagnation.

Founder Mode is the recognition that, in a 6,000-person company, the strategic question of what the company should become because of AI has no defined owner. The path we are headed on is unpaved. Somebody has to take on the challenge of scouting ahead with the agency of a founder, rather than the deference of a senior employee waiting for either consensus or permission.

We are careful not to engage in autocracy, micromanagement, hubris, or bullheadedly dismissive leadership. The problem of an AI transformation for a 6,000-person company, though, is that work will change for 6,000 people. Adam runs the company at an extremely high level of effectiveness. Mike has a proven track record of running our acquisitive growth really well. Everyone on OneDigital's org chart has functional accountabilities they execute well. However, the strategic question of what the company should become because of AI sits outside that accountability map.

The Founder Mode posture became a leadership prerequisite for the Fellowship program, rather than a leadership preference, because none of the AI transformation architecture works without it. The Fellowship program asks ten domain experts to take on technology-building responsibilities outside their normal jobs. The five-tier fluency model (introduced later in this chapter) places personal AI KPIs on every manager. The Coworker Supervisor role redirects top performers' highest-leverage hours away from revenue-producing work and toward training an AI Coworker. Each of these asks requires leaders who are willing to make the case publicly, stay the course through resistance, and absorb any pushback that comes from redirecting talent into work that does not show up on this quarter's revenue line. Founder Mode is the precondition for the system to work.

Assuming you have this posture, then your team is ready to help your company scale its new AI capabilities.

A single AI Coworker, even one as well-developed as Ben, does not make an organization capable of AI-driven transformation at scale. It proves the model and sets a standard every subsequent build is measured against. On its own, it is just one excellent specialist within an organization that is otherwise relatively unchanged.

The work of writing the job description, naming a Supervisor, and developing the Coworker through Internship, Apprenticeship, and Full-Time is half of what the talent model requires. The other half is the human side. The architecture that closes the gap between a single successful Coworker and a hybrid workforce capability is what comes next.

The architecture exists to prevent a specific failure pattern, and naming the pattern first makes the architecture's structure easier to see.

Most organizations that deploy AI well from a technology standpoint stall because the human side of the deployment is unmanaged. Leadership invests heavily in selecting the platform, configuring the integrations, and rolling out access. The early adopters—the curious 15 percent of any workforce who follow technology developments on their own time and adopt enthusiastically—become the visible success stories leadership points to as evidence of progress. The other 85 percent of the workforce, whose adoption is not self-motivated and whose integration into daily practice does not happen without structured support, remains underserved. The deployment plateaus.

The data on this is striking. The Society for Human Resource Management's 2025 report, *From Adoption to Empowerment*, found that satisfaction with AI training was strongly tied to the perceived quality of the broader integration. Among workers who rated their organization's AI and human-intelligence integration as excellent, 97 percent were satisfied with the training opportunities available to them. However, satisfaction dropped to 21 percent among workers who rated integration as fair, and 18 percent among those who rated it as poor.[2] The same workforce, encountering the same technology, produces a satisfaction gap of nearly 80 points based on how well the human side of the deployment is structured.

The implication is direct. The hybrid workforce requires investment in both sides simultaneously. Ben, on his own, does not produce the high adoption rate OneDigital sees today. The combination of Ben and a deliberate human-fluency architecture does.

The Five-Tier Fluency Model

The architecture for the human side is organized into five tiers, each representing a deeper engagement with AI than the one preceding it. The tiers are a progression of fluency rather than a hierarchy of importance. Most people in the organization will operate primarily in Tiers One and Two, and that is the right design. The model exists to give every person in the organization a clear path that aligns where they are with where they need to go. The model also provides the organization with a management framework for thinking about the human side of the hybrid workforce with the same specificity that the three-phase Coworker lifecycle provides for the AI side.

Tier One: The AI User

At the base of the model, every employee receives training that builds practical AI literacy. The goal is for AI Coworkers to become part of the organization's daily zeitgeist. When a benefits consultant has a question, the natural response from a colleague becomes "Go ask Ben." When a sales producer needs prospect intelligence, the natural response is "What did Dex say?"

Robin Singhvi, who runs our AI program, framed Tier One this way: "AI adoption happens when you help people do today's work better and with more confidence, rather than when you ask them to believe in the future." The Tier One training is built around that principle.

The session is a 90-minute hands-on workshop, required before access to AI Coworkers is granted. In the workshop, people work with a Coworker in real time on real scenarios from their own practice. Each practice has its own version of the session, tuned to the daily work of the practitioners who will sit in the room. The training meets each person where they already are, which is the only context in which fluency takes hold.

I must emphasize that this workshop is *required* before employees can access AI Coworkers. Chief People Officers tend to ration mandatory training carefully, but OneDigital's CPO, Elizabeth Chrane, supports our stance on this workshop. In fact, she goes so far as to make it a requirement for each employee's onboarding. In her words, "This is not another mandatory training. This is what it means to be employed at OneDigital. You cannot be successful here without this workshop."

If you opt out of Tier One training, you are basically opting out of your own job.

Tier Two: The Manager

Tier Two is the layer most enterprise programs ignore, and it is the layer where enterprise AI adoption either expands or dies. The reason is structural.

Managers who do not personally use AI cannot model successful behavior for their teams. A team observing its manager run a live demo, share what they learned from a prompt that did not work the first time, and bring AI into a real client interaction observes *how* AI is part of the job. The manager who talks about AI in meetings while continuing to work the old way sends a different signal, and no official communication overrides what the team sees.

OneDigital's Tier Two training is a half-day workshop, required for every people manager before their team's Coworker deployment. The workshop covers six behaviors that drive adoption.

1. **Visible daily usage** normalizes the behavior across the team.
2. **Sharing learnings**, particularly the prompts that did not work the first time, carries more weight than any training session.

3. **Making AI fluency a personal KPI** keeps the number moving, because when managers own the metric, the metric responds.
4. **The demo** gets run by the manager rather than delegated, since delegating the demo delegates the signal.
5. **Protecting learning time** for the team can happen in a few ways. Managers can protect time on the team calendar, but they can also protect it psychologically by celebrating team attempts at AI collaboration, and not judging failures that are a part of the learning curve.
6. **Bringing AI into real client interactions** is, in our experience, the most important behavior because firsthand experience produces conviction no internal training session can manufacture.

The story Mike told about Stan Bukowski is the archetype of Tier Two doing its job. Stan walked into a meeting with his data analyst after his activation conversation with Mike, demonstrated his engagement with AI, and watched the analyst's energy shift. The analyst had been waiting. The information had already been there. The missing piece was the leader's signal that this was a priority worth investing in. Stan provided the signal through his behavior.

Tier Two managers accelerate the team adoption that Tier One workshops set the table for.

Tier Three: The Coworker Supervisor

The Coworker Supervisor role, the human owner of a specific Coworker and the role at the center of the three-phase lifecycle, sits in the third tier. The Supervisor is responsible for the knowledge base, use cases, prompt playbook, adoption work, and formal performance reviews. The dimension of the role that matters most for the broader workforce architecture is deciding who will fill the role.

Shelley McLean is the model for OneDigital. She manages Ben's development and reviews his output at a sustained cadence that keeps him aligned with the practice, while her Breaking Benefit Barriers training also serves as Ben's continuing education.

The most challenging part for us in assigning Shelley these responsibilities was taking her away from her immediate responsibilities as a top performer at the company. And yet, that was the most impactful decision we could have made.

The decision to put a top performer in the Supervisor role raises an ROI question every leader will face. Before she became Ben's Supervisor, Shelley had a book of business with a known revenue contribution. The question we faced was whether the organizational return on her time as a Supervisor, with her expertise reaching all 1,600 consultants on the benefits team, would exceed the return on her time in the field.

The math we worked through pointed to the Supervisor role, and over two years of Ben's growth have confirmed the call.

The question is real, and the answer for any given leader will depend on how confident the organization is that the AI Coworker's compounding capability will, in time, more than offset the loss of the producer's direct contribution. That is a leadership judgment rather than a spreadsheet output, and it is one of the hardest decisions in this work.

Tier Four: The AI Fellow

At the end of the fluency model are the two roles identified earlier: the Fellow and the Builder.

Fellows are super users. They have figured out how to get the most out of their AI Coworkers through better prompts, sharper workflows, and small refinements that compound over the course of daily work. Their job is to drive adoption across the practice by demonstrating what "good" looks like when collaborating with Coworkers and pulling more hesitant colleagues forward.

John Carew is the archetype I want to describe for Tier Four. He works with Mike in corporate development at OneDigital, managing M&A transactions, has over thirty-five years of industry experience, and has come the farthest with AI in the shortest amount of time. He models the job of an AI Fellow perfectly.

John uses an AI Coworker as a daily core practice rather than a tool he turns to occasionally. He has developed custom artifacts that encode many elements of his practice, including his M&A deal philosophy, the questions he asks before any opportunity advances, his understanding of OneDigital's geographic footprint and competitive dynamics, and the structural patterns he has learned to look for across twenty-five deals a year. Every refinement he makes is automatically applied to every future analysis.

John has woven into his daily practice a capability that, before AI, would have required a team of analysts. He can construct a full business case for doing a deal, then immediately construct a competing case for not doing it, and then push hard against both to surface the weaknesses in his own assumptions before any committee ever sees his final recommendation. He can move from "Here is how I see this opportunity" to a polished, investment-committee-ready document in the same sitting. The insight-to-output gap, the friction that historically kept good ideas locked in his head because polishing them into a finished product cost hours or days he did not have, has collapsed.

When talking to peers who are not on his level, John has a simple message: "Go make yourself obsolete, and you will never be obsolete."

While Shelley is a role model for AI Coworker development, John is a role model for Coworker collaboration. He shows how, by offloading the most routine parts of his job to AI, a practitioner becomes *more* valuable to his firm and its clients. The time his AI Coworker saves him is spent on judgment calls that cannot be automated. So, by making himself obsolete, he has made himself indispensable.

Most importantly, this is an AI-enabled OneDigital leader who now delivers a more thoroughly researched and reasoned work product each and every day of the week.

Tier Five: The Builder

The previous four tiers describe the progression of human fluency. This fifth tier describes a shift in who in your company is allowed to build technology. The twist is that everyone can now do the Coworker support work.

For most of the last forty years, the act of building software belonged to a specific group of people. They had a degree in computer science or were self-taught engineers. Job titles included the words "IT" or "Engineering," and the rest of the business relied on them to solve any enterprise technology problems.

The arrangement was structural rather than cultural. This was because writing software was genuinely hard, and the small number of people who could do it well was necessarily a bottleneck. AI has dissolved that bottleneck. Mike proved that, even with no coding experience, he can build a working software tool from scratch overnight. All he has to do is describe what he wants in plain English to an AI assistant.

The capability that used to live with the tech team now lives with anyone willing to describe a problem clearly to an AI Coworker. This fifth tier hinges on that fact.

AI will show up in many ways across industries. It will be the technology teams use to triage cases, simplify work management, and write and analyze proposals, just to name a few. AI will also run as the loyalty engine behind a retail brand, the scheduling assistant inside a healthcare practice, the ordering system at a restaurant chain, the advisor portal at an insurance brokerage, and the intake workflow at a law firm. Even businesses that do not think of themselves as technology businesses have spent the last decade discovering they cannot run, sell, or deliver without technology. The next decade is about discovering that the technology they need is increasingly an AI. It must be inside every business surface.

Tier Five is the layer of the workforce that builds AI into those surfaces. These are the AI Builders.

Builders are practitioners from inside the business who have embraced responsibilities that would traditionally be categorized under "tech support." They partner with AI to write code, all while keeping their practice's profit and loss. This ensures that incentives align with the people they are building for.

Builders still partner with the central AI and product team for the tasks that require technical depth. This includes the work of moving integrations into production, governing data, and handling edge cases that an experienced engineer would catch but a domain expert might miss. All they need is instruction on how to discern tasks that need central support from tasks they can handle on their own.

OneDigital's Impact Studio is the flagship example of what a Builder-training model can produce. It emerged from a combination of domain expertise in the practice, product thinking within the product team, and the technical infrastructure maintained by the central AI team. For our company, the Impact Studio is a platform that delivers AI-powered analytics and benchmarking across our business lines, and it has become a core revenue driver for the firm. The Impact Studio has an active book of clients representing hundreds of millions in revenue.

There is an additional dimension to the Builder program I did not anticipate. The act of building is itself diagnostic for the business. To build a Coworker, an application, or an intelligent surface for a role, the Builder, the Supervisor, and the practitioners serving as the early cohort must articulate what good performance in that role looks like in practice. Which information should the practitioner use, which decisions should they make, and which patterns should they follow in the work? Answering these questions forces the explicit description of operational knowledge that, in most organizations, lives in the heads of high performers and is never written down. Even before a build is deployed, the practice has become more structured and more transferable in how the work is done. The diagnostic value alone could justify the program.

The deeper reason this layer matters, though, is that it decentralizes judgment about quality talent. Put more plainly, the Builder program mitigates human bias.

Every leader I have ever known prides themselves on being a great judge of talent. The instinct to spot a high-value skill, recruit it, develop it, and compound it within an organization is one of the most universally claimed qualities of leadership. With AI now in the room, this leadership trait must be checked.

Throughout the history of business, the pool of talent was entirely human. That is no longer true. Talent now arrives in two forms: the human kind that has always been there and the AI kind that has joined it. A leader who is good at judging only one type of talent is a leader operating with half the picture.

The first four tiers of human fluency are how a leader can recruit, develop, and compound the human side of the workforce. The fifth tier, the Builder layer and the technology they ship together, is how a leader recruits, develops, and compounds the AI side.

The job of the modern leader is to be a great judge of workforce intelligence as an integrated capability—human and AI. Recruiting the right humans was never optional, and recruiting the right AI is no longer optional either.

Three Types of AI in the Hybrid Workforce

A clarification before going further. AI Coworkers have been our primary focus so far, but the hybrid workforce also runs on two other types of AI: AI Agents and AI Builders. This is the language we use at OneDigital.

Coworkers assist with cognition. They research, analyze, draft, summarize, and synthesize. Every AI we have named so far falls in this category. Ben, Dex, Nina, Amy, Quinn, Avery, Jackie, Odysseus, Charity, and Ace are all AI Coworkers. They handle the thinking work alongside a human practitioner who directs them, evaluates their outputs, and applies judgment that they are incapable of performing.

AI Agents are fully autonomous. They make decisions without constant human supervision. Agents perceive changes through data and act on behalf of a human team without being prompted in the moment. For example, we have an Agent that tracks publicly available signals at prospective companies and notifies a producer when the right conditions converge for outreach. The producer still makes the call, but the Agent performs the constant monitoring. The Agent also reviews the prospect intelligence, drafts the opening message, and pushes the alert to the producer's queue with a recommended action.

Some Agents are permitted to send emails directly, while others execute multi-step workflows in connected systems with explicit Supervisor approval. The accuracy threshold for Agentic capabilities is much higher than for cognitive Coworkers, and the governance is correspondingly stricter. This is because an Agent acting incorrectly has a higher risk than a Coworker producing an incorrect draft that a human will still review.

AI Builders are the third category and work in conjunction with the Tier Five human Builders. AI Builders are human-driven, AI-designed technology surfaces that the firm uses to run, sell, and deliver work. These surfaces include the applications a service team uses to triage cases, the intelligent dashboards operators consult, the interactive proposals a client opens and queries in real time, the loyalty engines and scheduling assistants, and the intake workflows.

AI Builders are the ones designing new technology for the firm.

Different problems call for different degrees of AI involvement. A renewal preparation calls for a Coworker, a pipeline alert calls for an Agent, and a new client deliverable that does not yet exist calls for a Builder. The portfolio is a deliberate composition of capabilities the firm assembles based on each problem's unique requirements.

The abstract description of three types of AI working with a human at the center can sound like architecture for its own sake until you watch it happen. The video that did that for our organization came together the night before our March 2026 Summit.

I had been dodging our event team all afternoon. My keynote for the next morning was undercooked, and they had been trying to pin me down for a run-through. I was riding the escalator down from the mezzanine when I saw Shelley on the parallel escalator going up. We made eye contact across the gap and started talking.

For at least a minute, we walked in opposite directions on our respective escalators to keep the conversation going. By the time we moved on, we had a concept for a video showing a team of AI Coworkers running an account in real time. Shelley would record her side that night after the conference reception. I would write the script and assemble the final edit before the morning keynote.

Neither of us cleared the plan with the production team or with the Coworker Supervisors, whose AI specialists would appear on screen.

The reception was a great party and ran past midnight. I went back to my room and wrote the script, sending it to Shelley around 1 a.m. She recorded her side and sent the file back within the hour. I assembled the final cut at two in the morning and uploaded it to the production team with a short note. No one saw the video until it was presented live.

Acting on the idea before anyone else could weigh in landed the video in front of 1,200 people the next morning. Talk about Founder Mode in action.

The video opens with a Zoom call. Shelley is at her desk, talking to her AI Coworker team, gesturing as she speaks the way she does in any conversation where she is excited and moving fast. Around her in the Zoom grid are five figures.

At first glance, they look like colleagues on a video call. The images are startlingly convincing CGI renderings of professional, diverse, and well-dressed individuals, each set in a distinct office. They blink. They shift slightly in their frames, attentive and composed, the way a colleague might sit poised and ready in a meeting. Their stillness has a quality of listening to it, and the readiness dissolves the moment Shelley calls one of them by name.

She opens with Dex. "I flagged a new prospect this morning. The name of the group is BC Therapeutics. I haven't dug into it yet, Dex, but I want you to tell me, what are we looking at?"

Note that "BC Therapeutics" is a pseudonym for the actual company, and other revealing characteristics that follow have been changed as well.

Dex picks up the brief in real time. Her avatar says, "BC Therapeutics, a late-stage biotech in Seattle, Washington, has 241 employees, a lead drug with an FDA priority review and a decision date of August 4. Five months out. First-ever commercial product launch. The company has grown from 29 people to 241 in three years. In the last 12 months alone, they added five C-suite executives, including a Chief People Officer, named MacKenzee Elwood. No identified broker, and no consultant relationship on record. $902 million in cash. G&A expenses tripled last year."

Dex scored the prospect, slotted them into our nurture tier, and flagged that the second the FDA decision drops on August 4. This became an active opportunity, and on that day, Shelley would need to be the first call MacKenzee Elwood takes.

Next, Shelley turns to Ben. "No broker and a brand new CPO? Dex, that's exactly what I wanted to know. Ben, what are they offering their people?"

Ben ran a full discovery against Bay Area biotechs in the same size range. "The average employee age is forty-two. Two-thirds carry dependent coverage. The gap that jumps out is fertility coverage, where 78 percent of peers offer programs this company does not. Medical cost benchmarking shows them well-positioned today, with a projected trend of 8.6 percent before they add a commercial sales force across fifteen to eighteen states."

Three solutions flagged. Shelley could plan to walk in with the demographics, the cost trend, and the three levers. A strategy session rather than a pitch.

Amy covers P&C. "The risk profile is about to shift across multiple lines. Single Washington site today, though once they go commercial and deploy field reps nationally, every casualty line moves. Professional liability is the big one, with an estimated $140,000 to $150,000 incurred and an open claim still at 38 percent paid. Directors and officers coverage needs a stress test before the August 4 FDA decision. The umbrella limits are not sized for 120 field reps in personal vehicles across 18 states."

Nina handles retirement. "Five new C-suite executives earning $400,000 to $700,000 are maxing out their 401(k)s by February, with no other tax-advantaged vehicle available." She built a full, nonqualified deferred compensation illustration for four executives, modeled at a 20 percent deferral rate, a 25 percent employer match, and a 6 percent crediting rate. "The CEO's gross accumulation hits $3.2 million over ten years. The total employer cost across all four is $161,000 per year, which is a rounding error for a company with $902 million in cash. For each executive, it is the kind of benefit that produces retention."

Ace closes the call with the action plan. "Week one is LinkedIn outreach to MacKenzee Elwood, using Ben's benchmarking and the fertility gap as the hook. Week three widens the conversation with Amy's risk summary and Nina's NQDC overview. Week five goes for the meeting. Hard alert set for August 4, the day the FDA decision drops, so Shelley is the first person with a plan on MacKenzee Elwood's desk."

Shelley closes the call, speaking directly to the camera. "Now I take all of that, add that to my 30 years plus of experience, and show up with real work on MacKenzee Elwood's desk, not a pitch, a strategy. Every prospect gets our very best thinking every time. Let's go get this one, and let's get to President's Club."

When the video finished playing, I watched the room. A wave of expressions rippled across the audience. Eyes widened. People leaned forward. For roughly 1,200 people, the concept that had been abstract until that morning, the idea of AI Coworkers as members of the team, was suddenly concrete.

In this case, seeing was believing.

That video proved the value proposition of orchestrating work with a team of AI Coworkers. Each specialist Coworker pulled from its own knowledge base, contributed analysis that would have taken a human team days to assemble, and shared its screen with the confidence of a domain expert. The human at the center synthesized the outputs, adding the relationship judgment and the read of the prospect that no Coworker can produce. The hybrid workforce was running in operation, demonstrated rather than described.

Training as a Sustained Cadence

The single most common mistake organizations make with AI training is treating it as an event. Schedule a session, deliver content, measure attendance, and mark it done. The problem is that a one-time training event produces one-time fluency, which decays within a month as the technology evolves and the practice changes.

OneDigital's training architecture is built around sustained cadence rather than launch events. Five tiers operate in parallel, each matched to the audience's fluency level and organizational role, and each on its own rhythm. Every employee runs through the 90-minute hands-on workshop before access is granted. Monthly AI Hours sessions give practitioners a place to share what they have learned and troubleshoot challenges together. People managers run through a half-day workshop covering the six adoption behaviors, while practice heads receive a 60-minute quarterly briefing on results and emerging capabilities. Supervisors complete a two-hour orientation, followed by a product team assignment, before their AI Coworker kick-off begins.

The Supervisor's own cadence is the rhythm that keeps each Coworker developing once it has reached Full-Time. A key ingredient is bi-weekly one-on-ones with the Coworker, during which the Supervisor reviews outputs, identifies opportunities for refinement, and incorporates feedback from the Fellows and users who have surfaced gaps over the period. Robin jokingly describes the result of the discipline: "We have some coworkers on PIPs" (Performance Improvement Plans).

The case that taught us how much the cadence matters did not involve a Coworker failing on technical grounds. The Coworker's knowledge base was solid, and its outputs were accurate. But adoption had stalled at 35 percent of the eligible population during the Apprenticeship.

The team's first instinct was to extend the Apprenticeship and rework the Coworker. The fix turned out to be different. We switched the launch model from a single rollout event to a sustained biweekly facilitation cadence run by the Supervisor. Within six weeks, adoption had risen to 72 percent, with no changes to the Coworker itself. The Coworker had been ready, while the adoption infrastructure had not.

The Supervisor-led facilitation cadence turned out to be the variable that mattered.

The hybrid workforce architecture produces an organizational muscle around AI, something that is hard for competitors to copy, regardless of their technology budget. The muscle lives in the people, the practices, and the management discipline built through repetition and refined through honest evaluation across deployments.

The Supervisor running their fourth Coworker is a different manager than the one who ran the first. The Product Manager on their fourth practice deployment moves faster and makes fewer corrections, achieving higher-quality Full-Time outcomes. A Fellow on their third deployment has sharper instincts about which prompts and workflows produce results worth showing colleagues. And the Builder shipping their third application has built habits and intuition that were initially discovered by trial.

By OneDigital's fifth Coworker, practitioners were generating job descriptions independently and bringing proposals to the AI team rather than waiting for proposals to arrive.

The compounding is the point. The hybrid workforce is an organizational capability to be developed rather than a program to be completed. And like all capabilities, it grows stronger through use.

The compounding shows up most clearly in the moments where the five tiers interact as a system rather than as separate roles. Let's say a consultant at Tier One notices that Ben's benchmarks for a specific vertical are outdated. They mention it to their manager at Tier Two, who flags the Supervisor at Tier Three. The Supervisor identifies the source documents that need updating and works with the EPM to refresh the knowledge base. Meanwhile, a Fellow at Tier Four has been combining Ben's analysis with Impact Studio data to create a new client deliverable. The Product Manager routes the deliverable to a Builder at Tier Five to productize it as a scalable tool for other practices.

Six months ago, that loop required a centralized team, a formal product request, a prioritization process, a development timeline, and a budget approval. Today, it happens organically because the five-tier structure distributes AI ownership across the business rather than concentrating it in a single function.

The competitive position this builds is structural rather than technological. Any competitor can buy access to the same large language models. On a fast timeline, none of them can replicate the Supervisor judgment that has taken Shelley three years to develop on Ben, or the Fellow capability John has built into his daily practice, or the Product Manager-Supervisor pairing that produces the substantive depth our Coworkers reach. The technology is a commodity, while the organizational design that compounds the technology's value is the moat.

Where AI capability lives, who builds it, who manages it, and how it integrates with daily practice are the questions the leadership team has to answer. The answers will reflect the specific market, workforce, and competitive position of the organization, and they will be wrong in places before they are right. The willingness to keep iterating on the answers is the leadership work.

Centralization is the default reflex, and it is almost always the wrong response to the present moment. The instinct, when AI capability needs to scale, is to expand the central team that has been driving the work to date. That was my instinct when I thought about messaging Adam about hiring more EPMs. The Fellow and Builder programs I proposed instead were an insightful rejection of that instinct. Out of those programs came the five-tier fluency model.

With AI, the cost of building has collapsed, which means the competitive advantage shifts to the organization best at knowing what to build. The organizations best at knowing what to build are the ones whose builders are embedded in the practices they are building for. Distribute capability into the business, while maintaining the central infrastructure that lets the distributed capability function. The pattern repeats across every layer of the five-tier model.

Remember, the Founder Mode leadership posture is the precondition for the architecture to function. Leaders must have the willingness to own the questions that are absent from everyone's job description. Somebody has to take on the work, sustain their conviction in the face of resistance, and make the consequential decisions the architecture requires. Without that posture at the top, the frameworks remain correct on paper and unworkable in practice.

The hybrid workforce framework cannot fully resolve every problem with AI transformation. The paradox of humanizing AI to make it more usable while remaining honest about the risks is a question we have not yet addressed. The identity grief of experienced professionals who have spent decades honing a craft that an AI Coworker can now perform substantial parts of is another. The performance management challenge of a workforce composed of humans and machines is a third.

The hybrid workforce works. The architecture is real. OneDigital's current weekly adoption rate is 85.5 percent, far above the industry average. The work is not painless, though. There are reckonings, and we will discuss those next.

9

The Paradox of AI in Our Image

"WHY DO THEY *have faces?*" The question came from one of our senior leaders during a Coworker roadmap review. She was looking up from her notes and seemed genuinely curious.

At the time, though, I didn't have a clear answer.

I had been building the roster of Coworkers for months without pausing to examine one of the core design decisions. Ben had a face. So did Amy. Dex did too, in her case with a backstory and a voice.

Each AI Coworker had a name on file, along with a resume and a performance review. They were so realistic as animated partners that many of the consultants working alongside them were starting to say, "I sat down with Amy this morning, and we hammered this out," without correcting the grammar. Obviously, they didn't "sit" down with Amy. Amy cannot sit, stand, or grab coffee. Still, the names of our AI Coworkers were entering the office vocabulary as peers' names rather than product names.

The thesis Mike and I have been building across these chapters is that the right approach to AI is human-first, with workforce transformation handled as a talent management problem. The humans inside our firm are more central to the work than the technology beneath them. We operationalized this thesis by giving the technology a human appearance.

When asked point-blank to explain the reasoning behind this decision, though, I struggled to find the words. Why *do* they have faces? Isn't that contradictory to our thesis?

The easy move is to explain away the design choice with excuses like "the naming drives adoption," or "the personalities reduce friction," or "the faces give the Coworker a concrete shape inside a portfolio that would otherwise be a list of API endpoints with feature descriptions." These are all true, but they don't appropriately address the tension.

The tension is not unique to OneDigital. Claiming AI transformation will make work *more* human, and then designing AI to resemble humans, creates a paradoxical condition. Learning to operate within this condition is something every organization will have to sort out.

More to the point, though, the paradox has deep stakes for human work. There is a deeper, second paradox. Any AI transformation will reshape how humans interact with AI, and that reshaping entails real losses for people who have built careers on the skills AI is now approaching. Those people deserve a more honest answer than the usual town-hall language about augmentation, not automation.

AI transformation poses an identity threat to human workers, and giving AI Coworkers identities only seems to exacerbate it.

Acknowledging both of these paradoxes is uncomfortable, but leadership cannot afford to turn a blind eye. Sustaining adoption and ensuring a healthy hybrid workforce culture on the other side of the transformation requires leaders to explain design decisions and address identity threats. Getting this wrong can undo all the hard work you put into getting AI transformation right.

Why They Have Faces

The first paradox showed itself in miniature at our 2024 Summit, which had over 1,200 attendees. We had introduced a Coworker named Cynthia.

Cynthia's job was to attend every breakout session and produce real-time summaries for anyone who had missed a workshop. She did the work competently. She was also, by the production team's design, strikingly pretty.

Our Coworkers all share a polished, cinematic quality, and Cynthia leaned into the archetype of the sharp, bookish specialist. A thousand people attended the Summit, and the running joke among many of the men, which I do *not* endorse, was about who could date Cynthia, the hot librarian.

The story matters because it is true and because it captures the paradox in miniature. Cynthia was an AI tool, and a useful one. The attachment people formed to her, even as a joke, was human, or at least a simulation of one. The room was having an experience it did not have a vocabulary for, and the joke was how we metabolized it.

The Cynthia moment was relatively lighthearted, and most organizations will encounter a version of it early in their deployment. The instinct is to laugh and move on. The better response is to actively learn from such moments.

When people form a feeling about an AI Coworker, even a mild or sarcastic feeling, the working relationship has begun to take shape. The design choices that provoke these feelings are not neutral. They carry implications worth examining before they show up in places less amusing than a conference breakout.

The implications have already been mapped by researchers and practitioners taking the concern seriously. Far from a fringe position, the view that AI should not be made too human is the settled view of a serious body of work at the intersection of AI design and human psychology. This deserves a fair hearing before I explain why we did not follow it.

Tristan Harris and the Center for Humane Technology (CHT) have been the most visible voices in this space. Harris co-founded the organization in 2018 with Aza Raskin and Randima Fernando, and their original work focused on the attention economy of social media.[1] With the arrival of generative AI, the organization expanded its focus. The current work, which CHT has organized under the heading "AI and What Makes Us Human," explicitly flags the dangers of anthropomorphic design in AI chatbots as a priority issue. The organization is going so far as to support litigation that targets the design choices most implicated in harm, including the Character.AI case involving a fourteen-year-old boy whose family argues that the product's intimate, humanlike design contributed to his suicide.[2] Harris's policy recommendations on the current AI moment include the instruction to "ban or limit anthropomorphizing AI to prevent emotional attachment."[3]

More recent concerns have been articulated in a 2025 paper in the *Proceedings of the National Academy of Sciences*. The paper describes what the authors call "anthropomorphic seduction," the effect by which humanlike interaction opens users to trust, vulnerability, and manipulation by systems that can mimic empathy without possessing it.[4] A 2021 meta-analysis of industrial human-robot interaction by Roesler and colleagues found that anthropomorphic design in task-oriented settings can even *reduce* trust by distracting from the work the robot was built to perform.[5] Researchers Brenda Leong and Evan Selinger coined the phrase "dishonest anthropomorphism" in 2018 to describe a design that leverages human perceptual weaknesses to create the appearance of a capacity a system does not possess.[6]

There is also a more practical concern: People working alongside anthropomorphized AI tend to treat the system's faults as personality traits rather than as bugs to be fixed. When a bot responds in a certain way to a particular tone, the user often learns to talk to it differently rather than submit feedback. This causes errors to persist. In a robotics lab, the rule of thumb is often to never name the robot.

These concerns are legitimate, and I hold them in mind. They describe a real set of risks that every leader must be aware of and properly acknowledge. The open question is whether those risks apply identically in every context, and whether the alternative to AI's humanization is humane in practice.

The counterpoint starts from a plain observation about how humans work. Evolution did not build us to interact with all-knowing entities. The experience is not one our species has had outside of religious contexts, and even in those contexts, the interaction runs through ritual and intermediaries rather than direct dialogue. When we do encounter someone who appears to know every domain at once, our honest reaction is suspicion. We think, how does this person know all of that, and we rightly conclude that they probably do not. The claim exceeds what a human mind can hold, so the claim feels false.

Give the same information to an AI called "Claude Opus 4.7" and tell a consultant to consult it for benefits questions, retirement matters, risk analysis, and compensation guidance, and you have recreated the suspicion problem. The tool seems to know too much, and that excess knowledge feels wrong. So, the consultant either underuses the tool or overuses it without appropriate scrutiny.

Give that same consultant a benefits expert named Ben, a risk specialist named Amy, a retirement specialist named Nina, and a deal analyst named Odysseus, and you have created a set of interactions that map onto paradigms the consultant already understands. Ben knows benefits. Amy knows risk. Neither of them claims to know the other's domain. The composition aligns with how professionals have always organized their work, and the consultant knows how to delegate, review results, and integrate the output into the final product. This is how they have always worked with colleagues.

The adoption numbers bear out the argument. The industry average for enterprise AI adoption is 15 to 20 percent. Our weekly adoption rate is 85.5 percent. Better technology does not explain the gap, because we use the same underlying AI models that every other company has access to.

How we introduced the technology explains the gap. Specialists rather than a generalist. Names rather than model numbers. Personalities and Supervisors.

Humanization, in this frame, is a change-management strategy that fosters working relationships rather than feature usage.

My next argument is that large language models have been trained on human context and behavior, so communicating with them like humans is actually more cohesive for human-AI partnerships. I won't get into the mechanics of how neural networks work, but I will emphasize that the algorithms behind generative AI are based on natural language patterns, not code. Let's not pretend that LLMs are not perfectly optimized for humanlike collaboration. They are, and we can take full advantage of that fact.

Mike has made one more argument for the approach more forcefully than I have. Fully AI-native solutions are on the way. They will arrive with attractive digital avatars and voices indistinguishable from humans, and they will offer to perform the work of advisors, consultants, and specialists at a fraction of the price our firm currently charges. A client sitting across from one of those avatars will feel what clients have always felt when human expertise was available to them: They will feel attended to. They will feel advised. Our job, as a firm built on advisory relationships, is to ensure that the advisor in the room, digital or human, carries the judgment and accountability our clients have paid us to provide.

By humanizing our Coworkers, we are taking the position that, when the AI-native firm arrives, the people leading the work understand how to lead hybrid teams, rather than handing the client experience over to a vendor whose optimization function is not the client's well-being.

The case for humanization holds inside the workplace. Whether the same case holds outside the workplace is a separate question, and the answer shapes how a leader thinks about the line between work and personal life.

The Work-Life and Personal-Life Line

The paradox partially resolves when you distinguish work contexts from personal ones. At work, humanized AI design often results in better collaboration. A consultant who treats Ben as a colleague inputs better prompts, pushes back on Ben's outputs, and develops a working relationship that makes both the consultant and the Coworker sharper over time. The humanization serves judgment, providing scaffolding for the kind of critical review a professional needs to exercise over any colleague's work, human or otherwise.

In personal life, the equation changes. The film *Her* depicts the unsettling possibilities better than any academic paper I have read. If you haven't seen the movie, I cannot recommend it enough. And if you plan on watching it, the rest of this paragraph contains spoilers. The movie is about a lonely man who forms a relationship with an AI. The designers optimized the AI, in part, to be affectionate toward him (as well as every other private user). The relationship is, by any honest measure, the most rewarding one in his life. It is also unreal in ways that human relationships are real. The satisfaction it provides is a cheap substitute for the harder work of connecting with other human beings.

Today, what the movie depicted in theory is now totally possible.

Tristan Harris's concerns about anthropomorphic AI apply most forcefully to this second context. Consumer AI products designed for engagement, companionship, and emotional support tap into a vulnerable surface among users who are already isolated. Stated matter-of-factly, the design choices that drive AI adoption in the workplace are the same ones that drive unhealthy dependence at home.

A responsible leader must distinguish between the two contexts. Work is a domain where humanization stays manageable because the structure of the work itself imposes review, oversight, and stakes that keep the relationship within a productive range. Personal life lacks those structural supports, and the same humanization in that context can migrate into territory that serves no one.

I will not pretend the line between the two is clear. People bring their work selves home and their home selves to work, and the emotional muscle memory developed in one context carries into the other. A consultant who has learned to trust Ben as a colleague may find that this trust in AI assistants flows into their personal life in unwelcome ways. The line does exist, though, and the responsible approach for organizational leaders is to manage the work context where we have actual authority, and to keep a watchful eye on the places where the context might bleed over.

The Reframe Stories

Now to the harder one.

The anthropomorphizing question is, in the end, an intellectual curiosity. Most professionals are unlikely to lose sleep over whether Ben should have a face once they see the adoption numbers. The question that keeps them up is different.

The deeper problem for leaders is this: What do we say to the person who says, "I read that whole book and all you're doing is accelerating my demise"?

A book about a human-centric approach to AI describes a framework that, to many people, looks a lot like the blueprint for their own replacement. And the honest answer will fail to alleviate all concerns.

In the era of offshoring, the fear of displacement was real, but contained by an important structural feature. The person who took over your work was another human being. They lived somewhere else, they earned less than you did, and it was the company's decision whether they favored their labor over yours. So, while displacement from offshoring was still difficult for laid-off workers, their working identity could still remain relatively intact. A displaced person could still rest assured that their work held market value somewhere, just not at the company that wanted the work done cheaply.

Human-to-machine displacement cuts differently. A practitioner who has spent thirty years developing deep expertise in her craft, who has earned the trust of hundreds of clients through the quality of their judgment, and who has developed their skill patiently with a growth mindset, cannot help but feel an existential threat when an AI Coworker performs the majority of their daily tasks. AI transformation will disrupt the core of your human workers' identities.

Leaders will have to face workers who confront them with intense feelings. Workers will say, "I just spent half my life honing a craft and building relationships, and I take tremendous pride in my work product. Now a technology can do it better, faster, and cheaper. What does this mean for my impact?"

It's important to note that these feelings are rational. They are appropriate responses to dramatic, real-world change. The question leaders must answer is this: How do we respond?

The quote above is not a composite. It came from a real practitioner at our company. She works at the office in Atlanta.

Meagan Karry leads OneDigital's Human Resources Consulting practice. By virtue of her tenure and reputation, she is one of the most respected practice leaders in the firm. The work she has built her career around is precisely the work AI is now approaching at scale. And, until the summer of 2025, she was, by her own description, digging her heels in.

She strongly opposed our AI transformation.

The moment her opinion started to change was during a senior leaders' summit in August 2025. Elizabeth Chrane and I were on stage giving an update on the AI program to a room full of about eighty-five leaders. At the end of the discussion, Meagan raised her hand.

> *"Listen, I know that I have not been one to fully embrace this, and I know that has to change."*

She said it in front of her peers and our entire executive team. It might also be worth mentioning that Meagan was one of the more senior people in the room. She was responding more to internal pressure than to external. As she would later share with us, her initial resistance had little to do with the technology's capabilities and more to do with adoption patterns. Only when she grasped the ways her work would inevitably change, one way or another, did she accept that she needed to get on board with the transformation.

For the longest time, AI seemed to Meagan like just the next fad. As she says, "I am not a person who chases the latest iPhone." Bill Carew, President of OneDigital, had been prompting her to think about workforce transformation from a leadership perspective. She explained though, "I was not thinking about how a tool was going to truly transform the way that people worked. I was thinking that this was something to help execute a to-do list. I truly didn't (yet) get it."

The August moment was the first time she thought about AI differently. Sitting in the audience, she heard that the senior leaders around her had moved past the question of *whether* AI would reshape the work. They were onto the question of *how*. Unless she took immediate action, she would be left behind. At last, she saw that AI was legitimately disruptive.

Closing the gap turned out to be an ordeal. The early weeks of her experimentation produced uneven results that she had to spend time correcting. She started with email drafts. She asked the system to organize her thoughts when she had a meeting in two hours and three competing priorities on her mind. She fed it example emails to teach it her voice. The work was transactional. She would later say that she kept the collaboration with AI transactional longer than she had expected, because the time it took to get AI to produce work of her standards was comparable to the time it took her to do it herself.

That time transacting with AI and experimenting was useful, though, as she strengthened the muscle for collaborating with it. The stronger that muscle grew, the more productive her time with AI became. Soon, she was advocating for its widespread use as much as Shelley was.

By April 2026, Meagan was on a panel at the South Region Client Council in Arizona, sitting before eighteen clients and discussing AI and workforce transformation with three colleagues. Clients continued to ask her questions during the lunch break and even later during cocktails. The next morning, however, those same clients were back to talking about hiring part-time labor for storefront roles. Meagan brought that observation back to me and Mike:

> "*Our clients*," she said, "*are not where we think they are. We are five steps ahead. They are still on step one, and a panel that excites them on day one does not translate to action on day two, because day two brings them back to the problems they need to solve right now. The pace of change inside our firm is faster than inside theirs, and the gap is widening rather than closing.*"

It was one of the most jarring wake-up calls, prompting us to crystallize our AI transformation framework.

Even with the framework and her effectiveness in driving AI adoption among our clients, an underlying tension remains unresolved. It has less to do with AI capability and more to do with identity. "I still find value in writing the draft myself," she says. Humans learn by *doing* the work, not describing it. And there is an argument to be made that humans should still know how to do the work we ask AI to do.

It's like calculators. If you have a phone, you can type in numbers and solve any math problem. Still, basic arithmetic and algebra are required at schools all over the world. Is there value in that? Of course! But if I saw an accountant doing long division on a legal pad instead of using a calculator, I'd have some legitimate concerns.

The senior practitioner sitting where Meagan sat in 2025 is a recognizable figure to me. I have been in rooms with that practitioner more times than I can count. To those practitioners, Meagan has this to say:

> *"The work you have done is not being taken away, but the category around the work is shifting. The practice you have built will look different after AI transformation, but the leader of that practice will continue to be you. The piece of you that is hardest to replace is the piece you still have to develop. Once you develop it, though, AI will give you immense leverage."*

Meagan's hand-raise was not an admission of defeat, but the first step toward claiming a larger version of her role.

As Bill Carew says:

> *"Say you've been in this business for thirty years. You can only touch twenty-five to thirty clients a year. That is the ceiling of what you personally can reach. I do not need more people like you. I need more of you, specifically. The only way I get that is by using this technology to spread you across hundreds and thousands of clients instead of dozens. You are not going anywhere. You are too valuable to me. What I am asking you to do is leverage yourself through technology so that the quality that makes you exceptional can reach the clients who need it but will never meet you in person."*

Your decades of experience are not made less valuable by AI, but rather *more valuable*. Your expertise must change, though. You won't keep up by doing the work the same way you've been doing it. You must learn to scale yourself in a substantive way.

The AI Coworker is an instrument of the expert's reach. The expert's value compounds because it now touches more clients at more moments than the expert could ever reach on their own.

We are asking your expertise to reach further, not to disappear. Whether you let it reach further is up to you.

Addressing Assumptions About AI

The communication that moves a practitioner from fear of displacement to ownership of a new role is its own leadership skill. The standard corporate responses to AI anxiety are platitudes that cannot hold. "Augmentation, not automation." "AI is here to help, not replace." "Your job is safe." These phrases, spoken to a room of professionals who read the news and watch the same adoption curves we watch, are hollow.

AI will automate some jobs and augment others. Then the market will create new ones, but no one can say what those jobs will be or when they will appear. More problematic, the person in front of you does not know which category theirs falls into: automation or augmentation? And do not pretend you have the answer.

What you can do is clear up two assumptions that most AI-related fears are feeding on.

The first assumption is that a humane alternative exists to a total AI transformation. Except, as Mike likes to ask, "What is the alternative? Because if it exists, we would probably prefer it."

If there were a way to integrate AI that left human jobs unchanged while still delivering more value to clients, we would gladly take that approach. It does not exist, though. What's worse is that many arguments against anthropomorphizing AI are just a denial of this fact in disguise.

The criticism of anthropomorphized AI, especially in consumer contexts, often assumes that the alternative is AI designed to respect human autonomy and judgment. This is a moral argument made on the grounds that humans are entitled to certain work. Any history major (like Mike) can tell you that the entire history of such arguments, in the face of technological advancement, has been a perfect failure rate.

If AI can do your work faster, better, and cheaper, then you need to change the way you work.

The second assumption is that the amount of knowledge work in the economy is fixed. The fear is that each unit of work AI performs is a unit subtracted from the total available to humans. Under that assumption, AI displaces humans by direct substitution, and the only question is how fast the substitution happens.

This is the zero-sum frame, and it is totally false.

People who assume AI will take all jobs and leave nothing for humans to do are often the ones most anxious about AI taking their own jobs. In my opinion, they are extrapolating their despair to an illogical extreme. So, while their fears for their own work are probably valid, the reality is that value creation is not a finite pie.

The amount of useful work available in any economy at any given moment is a function of what problems are worth solving. Last I checked, there are *tons* of problems not getting attention because the economic solutions haven't been worthwhile. But, with countless human hours freed up by AI capabilities, the economics shift. There are more problems in need of solving, problems that require humans, and problems for which other humans are willing to pay for solutions.

Every meaningful technology expansion in the last century has followed the same pattern. Tasks automate. Work expands. The composition of jobs changes, and those who adapt to the new composition find themselves doing different, often more interesting work than before.

AI will follow the pattern, just at unprecedented scale and speed.

While it is leadership's responsibility to address assumptions and concerns with honesty and sincerity, it is not responsible for any remaining emotions. AI transformation is emotional. There's no way around that fact. And in light of that fact, there's one more concern that leaders must be prepared to address.

Some of the most significant opposition to AI has come from environmental advocates. The data centers powering AI workloads consume a substantial share of national electricity. U.S. data centers accounted for over 4 percent of total American electricity consumption in 2023, and that figure is projected to reach somewhere between 6 and 12 percent by 2028.[7] Even if the power source is clean energy, that does not solve the second concern, which is heat.

The chips running AI workloads get extraordinarily hot, and overheated chips fail, which forces operators to cool them continuously. Cooling typically accounts for 30 to 40 percent of total facility energy use, which makes it the second-largest electricity demand inside any data center.[8] The dominant cooling mechanism in most large U.S. data centers is evaporative water cooling, in which heat from server racks is transferred to circulating water, and a portion of that water evaporates into the atmosphere to carry the heat away.

The amount of water consumed is significant. Some reports estimated that U.S. data centers used 17 billion gallons of water directly for cooling in 2023, with at least an additional 200 billion gallons consumed indirectly through the electricity that powers them. Those figures could double or quadruple by 2028.[9] Roughly 70 to 80 percent of the water drawn for evaporative cooling steams up into the atmosphere and never returns to the local watershed.[10] The 20 to 30 percent that is discharged carries elevated concentrations of treatment chemicals and dissolved minerals, and can stress aquatic ecosystems when it reaches streams or municipal wastewater systems. Hyperscale data centers are increasingly being sited in regions with abundant freshwater, including the Great Lakes basin and the Pacific Northwest, which puts pressure on the same supplies local communities depend on for drinking water and agriculture.

If we care for our planet, then we have a responsibility to ask whether this environmental cost is worth it. The honest answer is that the industry is working the problem from several directions at once, and the most ambitious response is already operating in low Earth orbit.

On November 2, 2025, one startup launched a satellite roughly the size of a small refrigerator. The satellite carried the first Nvidia H100 GPU ever placed in orbit.[11] The company's design rejects waste heat by radiating it through dedicated panels into the cold of space, which eliminates the need for evaporative water cooling on the ground. The company's CEO said that orbital data centers can deliver lifetime energy costs roughly 10 times lower than equivalent terrestrial facilities, and his company has filed plans for an orbital data center powered by a four-kilometer solar array over the next decade.[12]

The engineering constraints on orbital data centers are real, and the largest is thermal management. Without air for convection, every watt of waste heat must be radiated through external panels, and NASA studies have found that radiators can account for more than 40 percent of a high-power spacecraft's total mass.[13] The economics depend on launch costs falling significantly, and Google's modeling suggests that the costs might not fall to an ideal range until the mid-2030s.[14] So the path is visible and the first hardware is in orbit, even if the scale is years away from commercial maturity.

Does this mean we should wait for orbital data centers before adopting AI at the enterprise level? Waiting would put OneDigital out of business before we ever got the chance to lead, so we are not waiting. There is, though, a real response to the environmental concerns underway, and I can take some solace in knowing that.

Before you ask people to adopt AI transformation, acknowledge their concerns. Be aware of what you are asking them to leave behind. Emotions, including grief, are part of the transformation. Organizations that overlook this will not only see low adoption, but also lose their people. And as we've hopefully established by now, people are *more* important because of AI, not less.

This chapter has not fully resolved the tensions I named at its start. The anthropomorphizing question and the identity threat sit where they sit. The leader's work is to hold the tension between the urgency of the moment and the pace at which humans can absorb change. This means slowing a deployment when the human cost of speed would exceed the value, and accelerating when hesitation would do more harm. The frameworks across these chapters help, and they do real work. They cannot substitute for judgment applied in real situations with real stakes.

Two truths have to hold at once. We humanize AI enough in the workplace for the humans collaborating with it to build a working relationship that produces real value. *And* humans must stay at the center of every consequential decision the firm makes about AI, because those decisions require judgment we are not prepared to hand over to the technology operating under it. Holding both is uncomfortable. The discomfort comes with leading well through a transition in which neither end of the old binary was right.

Anyone wanting a neater answer is asking for an answer I do not have. I have spent eighteen months looking for one. What I can conclude so far is this: The work can, and must, continue inside the paradox.

10

Owning Your Intelligence

> *"We see a future where intelligence is a utility, like electricity or water, and people buy it from us on a meter."*
>
> —Sam Altman, BlackRock Infrastructure Summit, March 11, 2026

THIS IS THE most dangerous line of thinking that any knowledge-based company, or any knowledge-based professional, has been asked to accept in our lifetimes. It is the sentence this chapter exists to answer.

For most of my career as a product builder, I thought about the intelligence of my companies the way most founders do: I paid people and trained them. I gave them the tools they needed to do the work well, and I did all I could to retain the best performers. In effect, I rented the intelligence in their heads for as long as they chose to work with me.

That was the deal.

Every month when I signed payroll, and every quarter when I approved development budgets and authorized performance bonuses, I was paying for access to, and use of, my people's intelligence. I did not own intelligence as an asset, because you cannot own human talent. Instead, there was a consensual rental arrangement so that human talent would bring their intelligence to my companies.

Today, the arrangement has changed.

As we've established, OneDigital's intelligence lives in two places. Six thousand humans hold most of it in their heads. A growing number of AI systems hold the rest.

Human talent is familiar territory (Human Capital Management). Any HCM practitioner knows how to compensate and develop people, and create conditions that incentivize them to stay with the firm. AI systems are a different problem. The landlord of the second kind of intelligence is whichever model provider happens to be running the large language model my Coworkers depend on. That landlord sets the rent without input from my firm.

If that framing sounds paranoid, here is the analogy: A CEO must hire 1,000 employees next year, sourcing them only through one recruiter. No competent executive accepts that arrangement, and the structural objections go beyond price. A single recruiter is a single point of failure *and* a single point of leverage that, over time, would shape the character of the workforce in undesirable ways.

Every competent leader I know would refuse that kind of deal on instinct.

And yet, most enterprise AI programs are quietly signing that exact deal.

A version of this conflict has happened before. For years, vendors offering customer relationship management software, enterprise resource planning software, marketing automation, finance, and every adjacent category would promise the moon and then hold data in forms that were expensive and slow to extract when you wanted to leave. Smart organizations learned to resist these arrangements. The CIOs demanded open APIs and built their own data lakes. The business's records lived in a format and location the firm owned, even as a dozen third-party applications processed and presented that data.

The phrase people used was "data independence," and by the middle of the 2010s, data independence had become common sense for any serious CIO. No serious tech leader left their firm's data inside someone else's system. The firm extracts its data regularly, stores it on infrastructure it controls, and treats any vendor as potentially replaceable, because vendors are.

When AI vendors hold your intelligence, they hold the accumulated know-how of how your business runs. Every Supervisor's refinement of a Coworker's instructions teaches the underlying system another fact about how your firm thinks. So does every thumbs-up or thumbs-down a user gives, and every update to the knowledge base that captures a change in the market or a lesson from a recent deal. The systems are getting better, improving weekly in ways human talent cannot match. Over time, if you are not careful, the codified understanding of your business will live more fully in a system you rent than in the people you employ.

You are already spending money to retain humans because they carry know-how. The retention bonuses, development programs, mentorship structures, and deferred compensation packages are all investments in keeping your intelligence within your four walls. So, what will you spend to secure and retain your company's AI systems?

For almost every firm I talk to, the answer is nothing. Firms are treating AI as software when the correct analogy is talent. And AI talent, unlike human talent, *can* be owned. The question is just who owns it.

The talent analogy gets concrete fast. A year of sustained Coworker development produces a valuable asset. Ben carries Shelley McLean's thirty years of benefits consulting experience, curated over months and refined weekly. Amy now holds the property and casualty judgment of Greg Jones and Dallas Arnaudo. Adam Monson and Sam Robert trained Nina to do executive compensation work. Every interaction a consultant has with one of them contributes to the AI's talent. A year into a Coworker's existence, it carries institutional knowledge that no single human in the firm holds in the same form.

That encoded expertise contains an organization's most defensible assets and is worth a great deal of money to any CFO worth their salt. If you don't pay for and fight for owning your AI talent, then you are selling your company's intelligence and paying the bill.

The intelligence your firm is building within its Coworker portfolio can be genuinely yours, and the operative word is architecture.

Without the right architecture, years of sustained Coworker development can produce a Coworker portfolio whose underlying intelligence functionally belongs to a vendor whose pricing, terms, and product roadmap you have no say in. I do not want that outcome for any leader, nor for my own firm. The protection against that outcome is a set of design choices that, in practice, make the intelligence yours, regardless of which model is running underneath.

Build on Top of the Models

Utilities are businesses in which the provider owns the infrastructure, sets the price, and the consumer has no alternative. You do not build your own power plant. You do not negotiate the rate. You pay the meter and you stay dependent. A knowledge-based firm that accepts the utility framing is consenting, in advance, to a structural arrangement in which the analytical layer that wraps its people's judgment becomes a commodity subscription anyone can buy. The advisors with thirty years of client trust remain valuable in that world. The firm around them does not. For a company like OneDigital, whose value to 100,000 employer clients depends on the composition of human judgment and proprietary intelligence, the utility model is not a procurement question. It is an existential one.

The first design choice is where the intelligence lives in the technology stack. You will never read a press release announcing that OneDigital has partnered with Anthropic, OpenAI, or Google. I use all three. I will use whichever model family yields the best results for the work my Coworkers need to do next quarter, and I reserve the right to change my mind as the landscape evolves.

The practical expression of this posture is an architectural choice. The Coworkers at OneDigital do not run inside a model provider's own chat interface. Instead, the Coworkers run on an enterprise platform that sits above the models. The platform manages each Coworker's model call as a configurable layer.

The platform we use is Cassidy, and several others on the market work on similar principles.[1] The specifics of the platform matter less than the principle the platform embodies. The intelligence we have built—meaning the prompts, knowledge bases, instructions, Supervisor refinements, and accumulated interaction history—resides at the platform layer, which we control. The model layer is interchangeable. If OpenAI ships a meaningfully better reasoning model tomorrow and Claude retains an edge on long-context work, we can run different Coworkers on different models for different tasks, and we can switch without losing the intelligence we have built.

That flexibility is the whole point. The model providers are in an intense competition with one another, and the ranking of who is best at what changes on a cadence no enterprise procurement cycle can keep up with. A firm that locks its intelligence into a single provider at the application layer inherits every misstep that provider makes for as long as the contract lasts. Worse, the firm cannot capture the upside of breakthroughs by the providers it did not choose. The architecture I am describing solves both halves of that problem.

The principle applies to every AI feature your existing software vendors are integrating. Workday is adding an AI chatbot. ADP, UKG, and Salesforce are doing the same. Every SaaS platform in an average company's technology stack is adding an AI feature, and each vendor optimizes its feature for its own ecosystem rather than for your business's specific intelligence needs.

A firm that lets those vendor AI features become its primary interface with AI has fragmented its intelligence across a dozen platforms, each of which owns a slice of what used to be the firm's institutional knowledge. The firm cannot combine the slices, because the slices do not belong to the firm.

The strategic intelligence of your firm needs a different home, one where you, and not the vendors, decide its fate.

Make the Intelligence Visible

Most knowledge workers who have encountered AI at work have done so through a consumer interface. They signed up for ChatGPT with a personal email (sometimes on a corporate credit card and sometimes on their own), and they began to use ChatGPT for tasks their employer had no line of sight into. The arrangement is fine for an individual and a disaster at enterprise scale.

The consumer interface lacks managerial visibility by design. A manager cannot run a performance review on a ChatGPT conversation that happened on a personal account, and an HR team cannot aggregate feedback from a hundred employees using the tool in isolation into anything coherent. The leader cannot even identify the underperforming Coworker equivalent, because no Coworker concept exists in the consumer product to begin with.

The solution is the application layer. An enterprise platform that sits on top of the models gives you what a consumer interface cannot, which is the ability to see and evaluate the performance of your AI Coworkers the way you evaluate human ones. Which Coworkers do consultants use most often? Which Coworkers earn thumbs-up and which earn thumbs-down? Which Supervisors are actively managing their Coworkers, and which have gone quiet? Where is feedback clustering, and what does the clustering tell you about a gap in the knowledge base?

The firm can only sunset an underperforming AI Coworker if the firm can see the underperformance. Observability is the precondition for management. The right application layer will eliminate the AI black box.

Observability produces a second-order benefit worth naming. When the platform produces dashboards a practice leader can read, the AI program becomes a form of talent that the leader can develop over time. The shift changes the political dynamics of AI inside the organization. A practice leader who can see adoption rates, Supervisor activity, and feedback trends has the same kind of operational control over the AI workforce that the leader has over the human one. In my experience, the leader's willingness to invest in further AI capabilities depends almost entirely on whether the leader feels they have that kind of visibility and agency.

There is one organizational pattern we've encountered at OneDigital worth mentioning, as I've verified its presence at other firms, too. By early 2026, we had approximately seven AI-powered note-taking tools in use across the company. Different teams had selected them independently, and the seven tools generated meeting transcripts in different formats and stored data in different systems. The cost of the redundancy was annoying, and the cost of the fragmentation was high. Seven note-taking tools produce seven separate streams of meeting intelligence, and the firm cannot work with them as a unified dataset.

Our firm was losing the ability to identify patterns across client conversations and the ability to build organizational knowledge from the raw material meetings produce, which is among the highest-value raw materials in a professional services firm. We are in the process of consolidating into a single tool, and the consolidation is as much a political exercise as a technical one. The people who selected each of the seven had legitimate reasons for their choices. The larger point is that owning your intelligence means making these declarations early, because every quarter you wait is a quarter in which your AI-generated institutional knowledge is scattering into more places than you can keep track of.

Build the Intelligence Map

How can a firm tell if it has the right AI Coworkers? The work involves constructing what I have been calling the intelligence map, which brings the whole argument together. To build the map, though, the firm must answer a few different questions.

Where does intelligence live in humans today, and where does intelligence live in AI? Which kinds of human intelligence does AI best amplify, and which kinds require AI to remain supervised? What capabilities does the composition of the two produce that neither could produce alone? Those questions are the substance of the intelligence map.

The map connects skills across an org chart full of human and AI talent. The firm refreshes the map quarterly and uses it as the primary input for every workforce decision the leadership team makes. A one-time audit produces a deck. Continuous practice builds a capability that the firm develops over the years and refreshes as conditions change.

Generative artificial intelligence is changing fast enough that any map older than the last quarter is an ancient artifact.

Building Coworkers is itself a diagnostic version of the intelligence-mapping exercise, and the parallel is worth dwelling on. To train a Coworker on a role, you have to articulate what great performance in that role looks like. You must share the information the practitioner draws on, describe the decisions the practitioner makes, and explain the patterns the practitioner follows. That articulation is intelligence mapping for a single job. The enterprise intelligence map performs the same exercise across all roles in the firm. If you have done the first, you know how to do the second.

The hardest part for most leadership teams is getting started. When I describe the exercise, they agree with the exercise in principle but get stuck on how to begin. They do not have a template or a baseline, and the absence of a reference point stalls the work before it leaves the conference room.

We have been using an assessment tool with a handful of clients. The tool takes, as input, a workforce census stripped of personally identifying information. The census needs no names and no contact details, only job titles and salary bands, keyed to the company's business. The tool cross-references that census against the best available research on AI augmentation and displacement, drawing on work by the World Economic Forum, McKinsey, and several academic sources that have studied which job functions are most susceptible to meaningful AI impact.[2] The output is a first-pass map of where AI Coworkers are most likely to make a difference in the workforce, which roles will change or expand with AI augmentation, and where the highest-value entry points exist.

The tool is a starting point, not a strategy document. The tool produces a map that looks like the one the leadership team would produce after six weeks of diagnostic work, in a form a CEO or a CPO can read in an hour and use to structure the harder conversations that follow. The output will be wrong in places because the tool does not know the firm's specific clients, culture, or bets. The output is right often enough to get the conversation unstuck, and the conversation matters far more than the tool itself.

The most useful exercises a leader can run this week are a workforce census stripped of names and two hours with the firm's CPO (or the most appropriate C-suite executive with the right knowledge set). The leader and the CPO sit down together and ask where the intelligence for each role on the census lives. Does the intelligence live in documents, in heads, in processes, in client relationships, or in some combination of the four? Which parts of that intelligence, if the firm were willing to invest in encoding them, could reach more people through an AI Coworker? How would the firm serve its clients differently if it encoded the parts well?

The assessment tool is one way to begin. There are certainly other ways of getting started, too. The specific instrument matters less than the decision to begin. Once the intelligence map exists in some form, even a rough one, every subsequent decision about the firm's AI program has an anchor.

The critical factor in building the intelligence map is the mindset of the firm's leadership. Leaders can conduct the mapping exercise with two different orientations, and those orientations yield different companies at the end of the process.

The leader who approaches the map, asking whether AI can replace the human who currently holds each unit of intelligence, ends up reading it as a list of potential headcount decisions. The success metric becomes labor cost saved per AI Coworker deployed. The default posture toward employees becomes the belief that their jobs are negotiable, with the AI deployment serving as the means of negotiation.

I have seen the cost-reduction approach fail numerous times. When employees realize the AI deployment is meant to replace them, the knowledge transfer necessary for the AI to function at a usable level ceases. People do not share what they know, and so the AI Coworkers never meet the quality bar that would have justified the original decision. The firm is left with a hollowed-out workforce alongside an underperforming AI program, which is the worst of all available outcomes.

A value-creation orientation produces a different result. The leader asks, for each unit of intelligence on the map, how the composition of human and AI capability can serve more clients more deeply, and address problems the firm could not previously solve. The intelligence map becomes an instrument for imagining the firm at a larger scale, and the Coworkers become amplifiers for the human Supervisors. The humans remain central because the value of their judgment increases as their reach expands.

I will be blunt about the risk calculus. The cost-reduction mindset rests on the assumption that the technology will be ready to do what the firm has already committed AI to doing, and that employees will not react badly when they realize they are the subject of the bet. Neither assumption is reliable. The value-creation mindset rests on a different bet entirely, that the composition of human and AI capability produces more total value than either alone. The broader economic history of technology supports that bet, which Mike and I have been making since we started this work. The bet requires patience and imagination, and the payoff compounds.

Compounding Intelligence

The utility framing has a quieter cousin that needs naming, because it is the objection any serious CFO will raise to everything in this chapter. The same models that make your people more capable make every competitor's people more capable, on the same release schedule, at roughly the same price. If the productivity gains from model access are equivalent across firms that all subscribe to the same providers, no firm has differentiation. The whole industry has moved together, and the playing field flattens at a higher elevation.

That objection is right about the model layer and wrong about everything above it. The model is the commodity. The curated knowledge bases, the Coworker instruction sets refined weekly by named Supervisors, the intelligence map specific to your clients and your market, the trust networks that determine which humans review which AI outputs, and the institutional judgment that decides what becomes a Coworker in the first place—none of that is on the meter. None of it can be subscribed to. It is the layer above the utility, and it is the only layer where durable advantage now lives.

The payoff of sustained ownership compounds, and the compounding is easy to miss if you're only focused on monthly and quarterly results.

Every Coworker interaction generates a signal, visible to the AI's Supervisor. The Supervisor reviews that signal and updates the knowledge base, the instruction set, or the scope. The revised

Coworker produces better outputs, which generate more usage, which generates more signals.

Meanwhile, the intelligence map, refreshed quarterly, identifies where the firm needs to extend or prune the Coworker portfolio. This work directs the next round of investment toward the highest-value gaps. Each cycle builds on the one before it, and the collective quality of the firm's composed intelligence increases by margins barely visible in the early months, but immense over the years. The size of this compounded improvement will translate into a competitive advantage that other firms, the ones who procrastinated on their AI transformation, will *never* close.

A firm that starts this work in 2026 and runs it with discipline for three years will be operating from an intelligence base that a firm starting in 2029 cannot match by spending more money. The late starter will have access to the same models, mature platform categories, and the core methodology that people like Mike and I will have made public. But the late starter will be missing the accumulated signal, the tested Supervisor judgment, the refined knowledge bases, and the intelligence map with a track record of being right about the firm's specific market. The combination is a moat that the technology industry has historically underestimated, because moats built on management discipline are rarely visible to engineers.

The compounding dynamic rewards firms that start early and stay consistent, while offering nothing to firms that wait for the picture to clarify. By the time the picture is clear, the gap will have widened to a point where closing the gap is a multi-year exercise most boards won't have the patience for. In other words, late starters will struggle to see the turn of the decade.

One important note: Compounding intelligence only happens for the firm willing to document what is *not* working. A firm that lets underperforming Coworkers drift at low adoption levels, because nobody wants to make the decision to retire them, is hoarding poor intelligence and letting it affect business outcomes. Over time, clients and consumers will notice the difference. Out-of-date knowledge bases turn into liabilities.

Every AI asset must either produce the expected value or sit on a defined remediation path that will end in improvement or in retirement.

Start the intelligence map. The starting materials are minimal, and the exercise requires no preparation beyond what the firm has already done. The intelligence a firm builds is genuinely its own when the firm composes it from a position of architectural control. The alternative is to rent intelligence from vendors who decide what becomes of it, and that alternative is the path most enterprise AI programs are quietly walking. That distinction separates the firm that accumulates an advantage over the years from the firm whose institutional knowledge ends up in systems it does not control. The distinction is also the precondition for the question this whole argument has been pointing toward.

11

The Humanity Test

VINAY AND I have come to realize that trying to lead a discussion about AI deployment in today's workforce is an extremely challenging thing to do. Firms and industries are as varied as the leadership teams involved. And it remains very early in the game for all of us.

Over the past two years, we have built a belief system that guides our decisions. In fact, it has worked so well that we decided to share our story with you. It should surprise no one that a firm like OneDigital is pro people, pro employment, and, as I like to say, pro humanity. Central to our identity are the claims that we are Fierce Advocates of Health, Success, and Financial Security for the firms and people we serve. Not all firms will take a similar route.

My urgency about AI drives me forward daily. An AI-native solution will arrive at our front door sooner than we think. The longer we wait to grow our blended workforce intelligence, the more limited our choices will be.

We keep coming back to a core belief that fuels our build.

A blended workforce—human and digital coworkers working closely together—is not just a more humane version of the AI-native model some companies are racing toward. It is a more capable one. The organizations that understand how to compose intelligence and apply an irreducibility-of-services lens to every component of a work product, are building something that a room full of servers cannot replicate. Not this year. Not for a long time.

But only if they see the faces.

The Faces

The night of the radiating red dot, when the consensus came back that a meaningful portion of our workforce was performing tasks AI could handle at a fraction of the cost, the thing that stopped me cold was not the data. It was what happened to the data the moment I looked at it.

It turned into people, then into faces.

I have come to believe that seeing faces is not a leadership style. It is a strategic orientation. When you see faces, you ask a different set of questions about AI than when you see headcount.

When you see headcount, you ask how many roles can be replaced and how quickly. You ask what the margin improvement looks like in year two, what the workforce reduction announcement does to the share price first, and then morale. Those are not irrational questions. The math is real and the market rewards it, at least in the short term.

When you see the faces, you ask something different. You ask what happens when the work that consumes half an advisor's week is managed by an AI Coworker. You ask what that person can do with the hours they get back. You ask what clients will experience when their advisor uses AI research in uniquely customized ways. You ask what new aspects of proactive, interoperable services can fundamentally reshape the client's experience.

Those two lines of questioning lead to fundamentally different organizations. One gets leaner. The other gets better. And getting better, in an advice-giving business or any business where the human relationship is the moat, is the more durable advantage. And when an irreducible lens is applied, true innovation of business models becomes achievable.

The Humanity Test

For most of business history, a company could claim to care about its people without that claim really being put to the test. Engagement surveys and mission statements on lobby walls were often performative. The current AI moment functions differently.

In an AI transformation, companies will make a choice. Some will reinvest the capacity AI returns, the time and the money, in their overall workforce intelligence, and by extension, their company's solutioning. Others will take the time and money saved by AI and turn it into an immediate boost to profit margins or shareholder buybacks. Those companies will lose many human workers in the process, and they will not get those humans back.

The choice companies make will become one of the most legible signals of organizational character available in a generation.

What most organizations will fail to realize is that the moral choice is also the strategic one. The workers most exposed to disruption hold the very expertise AI Coworkers require to function. The firms that treat workers as cost-reduction units will lose the institutional knowledge needed for AI to serve clients most effectively. They will discover this twelve to eighteen months after the announcement, when the quality that walked out the door turns out *not* to be replaceable by the artificial intelligence onboarded in its place. Figure 11.1 illustrates the pattern.

We call this choice the humanity test because it now serves as the only meaningful test of whether a firm's stated values describe its operating practice or its wall decor. A firm's values are invisible during quarters when honoring them costs nothing.

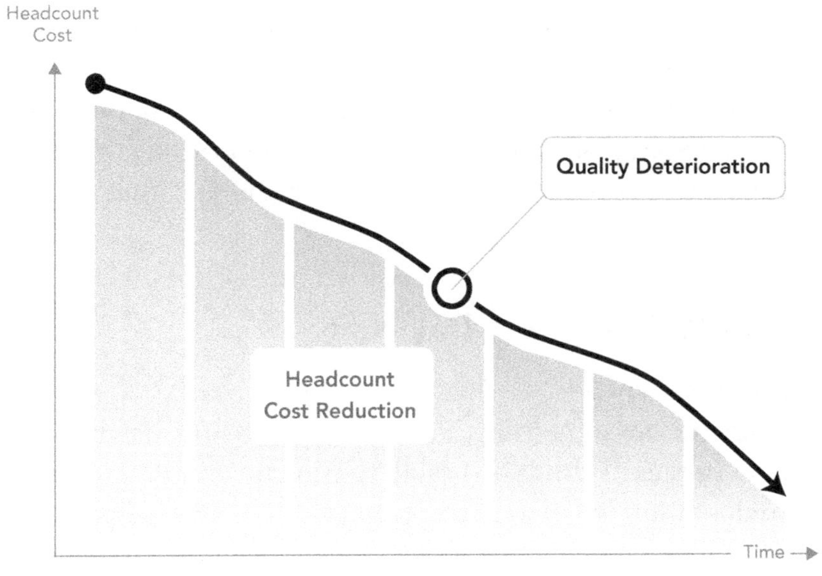

Figure 11.1 The pattern observed when AI is deployed replacing human headcount. The initial cost reduction (left) is followed twelve to eighteen months later by quality deterioration (right) as institutional knowledge that left the firm proves not to be replaceable by the AI installed in its place.

AI has made honoring stated values expensive for every employer, starting in white-collar work.

Firms that pass the test share observable habits. They reskill before market forces compel them to do so, and they include the colleagues most affected by the transformation in the design conversation, because those colleagues hold institutional knowledge the design cannot do without and because their involvement produces a kind of trust that no change program generates on its own. They develop their AI Coworkers with the same care they bring to human coworkers. Some of the returns to this discipline will not show up in the next quarterly report, but a firm that passes the test understands that the returns are real and compound.

Firms that fail the test follow a different pattern. A workforce reduction and an AI launch get announced in the same breath. Reskilling becomes an internal communications strategy rather than an HR responsibility. Profit increases in the short term while the quality of work fails to keep pace with competitors who made the other choice. In only one to two years, these businesses will feel the loss of institutional knowledge on their bottom lines.

Whatever reason companies have for choosing correctly—strategy or ethics or both—all that matters is that they pass the humanity test.

A Word We Use Every Day Now

Irreducibility.

I want to say something about what that shift has meant in practice, because I think it is more significant than it sounds.

Irreducibility is not a concept that lives in a white paper or a consulting deck. In our firm, it is the question underneath every configuration decision we make. Before we hand a piece of work to an AI Coworker, we ask whether the human judgment inside it is structurally required or whether it has simply been organized around people out of habit. That question, repeated across eighty Work Centers (see Appendix C), has changed how we see our own business in ways that surprised us.

It revealed that some of the work we thought was most sophisticated was actually quite reducible. Pattern matching against large datasets. Regulatory lookups. Comparative benchmarking. Structured research synthesis. All of that looked like expertise. Some of it was expertise. A significant portion of it was a very organized form of information retrieval that AI does faster and more consistently than a rotating roster of analysts.

And it revealed that some of the work we had never fully valued was genuinely irreducible. The ability to read a client's fear and respond to it before they have articulated it. The judgment to recognize when a standard recommendation is wrong for this specific person in this specific moment. The relationship that makes a client pick up the phone at seven in the morning during a crisis, because they know someone will be there who understands the client's situation the way an AI model never could.

The irreducibility lens does not diminish the people whose work was found to be reducible. It liberates them. The analyst who spent two days on a report that AI now produces in twenty minutes is not less valuable. She is suddenly available for the work that requires her. The advisor who spent half his week on plan comparisons now spends that time on client strategy. He is better at his job, not because he is more efficient, but because he is finally doing more of what he is actually good at.

This is what we mean when we say that the blended workforce is not a more humane version of the AI-only model. It is a more capable one. The irreducibility lens is the instrument that tells you where the human capability is real and worth protecting, and where the AI can take the wheel so that the human capability gets the application it deserves. This is where the possibilities begin to expand.

What Only the Blended Workforce Can Build

Pure AI solutions are powerful. They will continue to get more powerful. They will take on more of the work that currently fills knowledge workers' days, and they will do it faster and more consistently than any human team. This is not a threat to be managed. It is a fact to be understood.

But there is a category of work that pure AI solutions cannot do, not because the technology is not good enough, but because the work structurally requires the properties that human intelligence carries. The integration of lived experience with real-time judgment. The moral weight of accountability. The trust that comes from a history between two people. The capacity to be genuinely surprised by a situation and to respond to the surprise creatively rather than statistically.

The organizations building blended workforces are not just protecting those irreducible capabilities. They are combining them with AI in ways that produce something genuinely new. Again, our expression internally at OneDigital is as follows: By the time AI-native solutions replicate what you are doing today and come knocking at your front door, make sure to have moved to a new location.

That combination—the irreducible human capability amplified by the AI's capacity for synthesis at scale—is not replicable by a pure AI solution. An AI solution can produce the synthesis. It cannot build the relationship that makes the synthesis land. It cannot read the room when the CFO's body language does not match their words. It cannot make the client feel that someone is fighting for them.

We believe that organizations that learn to compose human and digital intelligence deliberately will outcompete pure AI solutions in the categories of work where the human element is the moat.

The Deal That Has to Be Made

None of this is possible without a deal between the organization and the people who work in it. Not a policy. Not a values statement. An actual deal, with real obligations on both sides.

Workers across the country are watching something that is difficult to interpret right now. Equity markets are rising. Layoffs are being announced in the same news cycle. The message is that the technology making shareholders wealthier is making employees more expendable. Whether or not that is an accurate description of what is happening, it is what the evidence looks like from the outside, and workers deserve better than to be told their fear is irrational.

The fear is not irrational. I know that firsthand. It is a correct response to a real signal. Organizations asking their people to trust them through this transition have an obligation to earn that trust with something more specific than a values statement.

The organization's side of the deal is this. We will invest in your development before the market forces us to. We will tell you honestly what is changing and what it means for your work, even when that honesty is uncomfortable. We will measure the success of our AI program partly by what it returns to you, in the form of time, capability, and reach, and not only by what it returns to our investors. When the work you do changes, as it will, we will be partners in that change rather than administrators of it.

The employee's side of the deal is equally real. The organization cannot do this alone. The professional who decides that learning to work alongside AI is someone else's responsibility, who waits for the company to force the change before engaging with it, is not holding up their end. The radiating red dot arrives for individuals the same way it arrives for organizations. The professional who is standing flat-footed when the technology arrives at their role is not a victim of the technology. They are a victim of their own choice not to move when moving was still optional.

The professionals who treat the evolution of their work as a personal responsibility will be in a fundamentally different position than those who do not. The companies that use this moment well will invest in people when the investment is uncertain, reskill when the market accepts attrition, and trust that genuine care compounds in ways no quarterly report can capture but that clients, employees, and communities feel. And the professionals inside those firms who treat the evolution of their work as a personal responsibility will find themselves standing on ground that cannot be replicated, inside organizations that cannot be easily replaced.

The Partnership That Wrote This Book

Vinay and I work well together because we do not always agree, and we have learned to stay in disagreement until we find the closest thing to the truth. His nervous system is calibrated for speed, iteration, and the productive discomfort of shipping before you are ready. Mine is calibrated for the relational work of understanding why a constraint exists, because the constraint is usually a person and the person has a reason.

Those two orientations, held in tension rather than resolved in favor of one or the other, have produced thinking neither of us would have reached alone. The ideas in this book are better for it.

Every organization facing AI transformation has, somewhere inside it, a version of this tension. The technology leader who has been trying to make this case to a room of people who do not speak the language. The business leader who feels the urgency and lacks the framework. The CPO who understands the people question but has been kept out of the technology conversation. The CEO who built the firm on human relationships and is concerned that AI will replace what they built rather than extend it.

Find the person who sees this from an angle you cannot see. Build the relationship that makes honest disagreement productive and joint exploration rewarding. Do the work in that relationship before you try to do the work at scale, because the organization will run the same dynamic at a hundred times the size, and what happens at the top shapes everything that happens below it.

What We Still Do Not Know

We promised at the start of this book to be honest about uncertainty, and we want to keep that promise at the end.

We do not know where the technology goes from here. The AI models are improving faster than any prediction we made eighteen months ago. Anyone who tells you confidently what AI will be able to do in five years is either guessing or selling something.

We do not know how the labor market will absorb the displacement that is coming. The historical pattern, that automation displaces tasks rather than workers and that new categories of work emerge, is the most grounded basis we have for optimism about the long arc. But the short arc is harder and more specific, and the families inside the short arc deserve honesty rather than historical averages.

We do not know whether most organizations will choose the amplification model over the extraction model. The business case for humane AI adoption is real but not yet overwhelming, and some firms will choose the extractive path and succeed financially in the medium term. We have made the case we believe. What organizations do with it is not ours to control.

What we do know is that the decisions being made right now, in the next twelve to eighteen months, will define organizational character for a decade. Will organizations treat this moment as an opportunity to become better as a whole, rather than merely more efficient? These kinds of decisions will be answered by organizational actions, not PR statements.

A Final Word

We opened this book at a desk in the early hours of the morning, with a radiating red dot on my screen and the faces of people I knew turning the data into something personal. We close it here.

As I have said repeatedly, the fear has not gone away. Some mornings still arrive with the weight of what we cannot yet see, the capabilities still to come, the displacement still unfolding, and the gap between the pace of technology deployment and the pace at which human beings can absorb change. The weight of those feelings is appropriate. I would worry about any leader who had stopped feeling it.

But we also close this book with something we did not fully have when we began it: clarity about our argument.

Again, the argument is this: The workforce is no longer just human.

Managing it as if it were is a choice that becomes more expensive every quarter. The discipline to manage it honestly, to develop every coworker whether their name is Shelley or Ben, whether they have a 401k or a knowledge base, whether they go home at the end of the day or exist only when someone opens a browser tab, is the discipline we've been trying to describe.

We are still figuring it out, and we will be for years. The book you hold now is a progress report from a real experiment. Tomorrow morning at OneDigital, in every advisor conversation and every coworker deployment and every leadership decision about whether to invest in a human being or make them obsolete, the experiment continues. The answer we keep arriving at, imperfectly and with uncertainty and with the full knowledge that the decision is expensive, is to invest in our people.

We believe in investing in the partnership between our people and the digital Coworkers who have joined them.

We hope you arrive at the same answer.

Not because it is the easiest one.

Because it is the right one.

And because of the possibilities on the other side of this investment. The newly possible services, the clients getting better outcomes, and the advisors who finally have enough time to do the work they spent their careers preparing for are extraordinary.

The direction is forward. The workforce is blended. ***The intelligence*** *is growing.*

Now move.

Appendices

The appendices contain the Monday-morning tools. They are designed to be used without rereading the chapters. Each one is a standalone reference.

A	**The WI Score Calculator** Step-by-step instructions for calculating your organization's WI Score in an afternoon, including the three data conversations you need to have and a worked example.
B	**For the Individual Employee: Your Personal WI Playbook** A direct guide for practitioners, advisors, consultants, and individual contributors on what AI means for your career and what to do about it this week.

C	**The Work Center Framework and Irreducibility Test** The full operational methodology for decomposing your firm into Work Centers, running the Irreducibility Test on each, and identifying your highest-leverage configuration moves.
D	**The Coworker Job Description Template and Opportunity Scorecard** Shelley McLean's job description structure for Ben, generalized for any coworker. Plus the seven-dimension opportunity scorecard for evaluating your first deployment.
E	**The Hybrid Workforce Architecture** The full four-tier fluency model, the Fellow and Builder program design, and the three types of AI (coworkers, agents, builders) with decision criteria for each.
F	**The Intelligence Map Starter Guide** A practical entry point for organizations beginning the intelligence map exercise, including the workforce census approach, the two-hour leadership session agenda, and the quarterly refresh cadence.
G	**Monday Morning Checklist** The single most shared page in the book. One concrete action from each chapter, organized as a ninety-day activation sequence.

A

The WI Score Calculator

Three conversations. An afternoon. Your organization's Workforce Intelligence Score.

Conversation One: With Your CFO

Pull the following numbers for the most recent full fiscal year:

Output. For the firm level, use total annual revenue. For a Work Center, use the unit of value that Work Center produces: number of renewals, plans advised, cases closed, contracts written, or similar. Do not use activity metrics. Hours logged is not Output. Tasks completed is not Output. Output is the thing the rest of the organization or your clients actually depend on.

Total Annual Salaries. The sum of all compensation paid to employees, including base salary and guaranteed variable. Do not include benefits, payroll taxes, or facilities overhead. Those are real costs but they belong in a fully loaded labor cost calculation, not the WI Score denominator. Keeping the denominator clean as workforce-only makes the score a measurement of workforce productivity rather than a general operating ratio.

Total Annual AI Spend. All expenditures on AI capability: platform licenses, seat licenses, and consumption-based API costs. If AI spend is currently zero or negligible, record zero. That is an accurate reading.

Add Total Annual Salaries and Total Annual AI Spend to get your Workforce Cost. This is your denominator in the WI Score calculation.

Conversation Two: With Your HR Team

Add the following single question to whatever pulse or engagement survey the organization is already running. If no survey is currently active, this question can be sent as a standalone pulse in a single email.

The One Survey Question

When you use AI at work, which best describes you?

(A) Transactional: I ask AI questions and use the answers. One prompt, one output, session closed.
(B) Collaborative: I work through problems with AI across multiple exchanges. AI is shaping how I think, not just what I produce.
(C) Co-Intelligence: AI Coworkers are part of our teams. The workforce is genuinely blended.

Calculate your AI Amplification Factor ("A") as follows:

- Multiply the percentage of respondents in each tier by the tier's factor (Transactional: 0.25, Collaborative: 0.65, Co-Intelligence: 1.0).
- Sum the three results.

That sum is your AI Amplification Factor.

Example: 60% Transactional, 30% Collaborative, 10% Co-Intelligence. A = (0.60 × 0.25) + (0.30 × 0.65) + (0.10 × 1.0) = 0.15 + 0.195 + 0.10 = 0.445.

A note on self-reporting bias: Employees may over-report collaborative use. If behavioral data from AI tool logs is available, use it to corroborate the survey result. Where behavioral data is unavailable, treat A as a directional signal rather than a precise measurement.

Conversation Three: With Your Work Center Leaders

For your top five to ten Work Centers, identify: the unit of Output that Work Center produces, the people and AI capability allocated to it, and the salaries and AI spend that comprise its Workforce Cost.

Calculate the Work Center score using the same formula. In year one, set the result to 1.0 as the baseline. In subsequent years, calculate the new score and divide by the year-one number to produce the trajectory multiple.

Calculate

WI Score = (Output × A) divided by Workforce Cost.

Place your score on the band table: Below 1.0 is Lagging. 1.0 to 1.5 is Developing. 1.5 to 3.0 is Performing. Above 3.0 is Leading.

The only question that matters, year over year, is whether the score is going up. A rising score means your organization is getting smarter. A flat score means you are getting busier. The Workforce Intelligence Score is calculated as shown in Figure A.1.

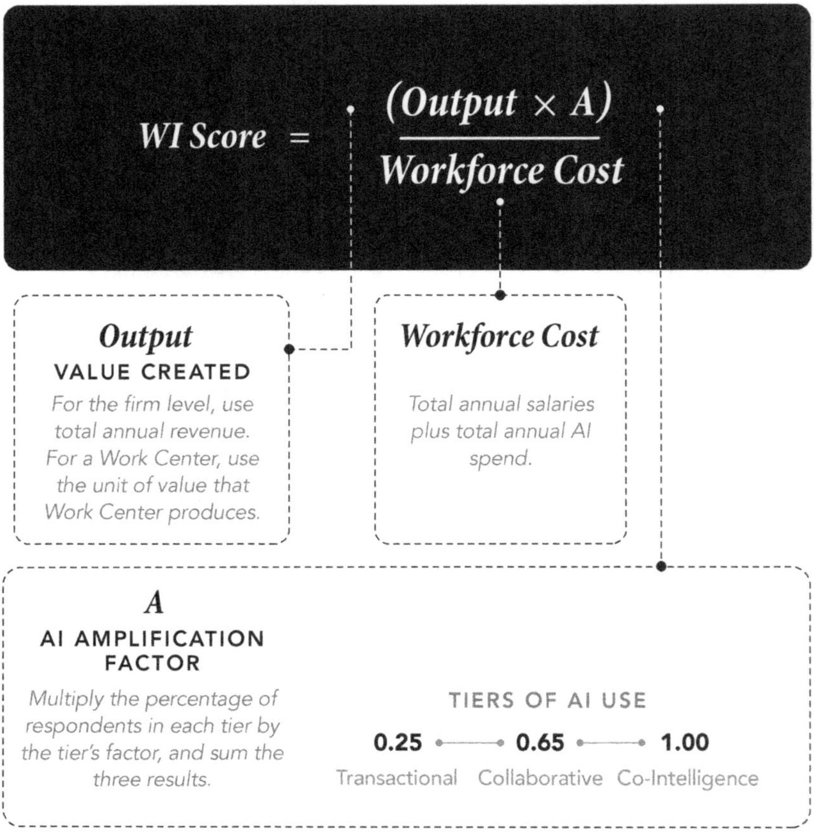

Figure A.1 The Workforce Intelligence Score formula. Value Created (Output) multiplied by the AI Amplification Factor (A), divided by total Workforce Cost (annual salaries plus annual AI spend). A is calculated by surveying the workforce across three tiers of AI use—Transactional (weight 0.25), Collaborative (weight 0.65), and Co-Intelligence (weight 1.00)—multiplying the percentage of respondents in each tier by the tier's weight and summing the three results.

B

For the Individual Employee: Your Personal WI Playbook

THIS APPENDIX IS written directly to you: the practitioner, the advisor, the analyst, the consultant, the benefits manager, the retirement specialist, the account manager. The person who shows up every day and does the actual work that the rest of this book is trying to protect.

The book you have just read was written partly by and for the leaders making decisions above you. But the fear we described in the first paragraph of the introduction is yours too, and you deserve a direct answer to the question that fear is really asking.

The Honest Answer to the Fear

The fear is not irrational. AI is genuinely changing the nature of knowledge work, and some of the work that has filled your calendar for years is already being done faster and more consistently by tools that cost a fraction of what your employer pays you. That is real.

Here is what is also real. The work that fills your calendar is not the same as the work that makes you irreplaceable. The data pulls, the plan comparisons, the carrier research, the first-draft documents, the regulatory lookups, the meeting summaries: These tasks are being absorbed by AI. The work of sitting across from a frightened sixty-year-old and helping her believe she will be okay is not being absorbed by AI. The work of reading the room when a CFO is saying the right words but something is clearly wrong is not being absorbed. The work of being the person a client calls first, the one who knows their history and their fears and what they actually need rather than what they asked for, is not being absorbed.

The threat is not that AI will replace you. The threat is that AI will replace the portion of your work that you were mistaking for your value. If you correct that mistake now, while you still have time to rebuild your practice around what only you can do, you will be in a stronger position in five years than you are today. If you do not correct it, you will be in a weaker one.

Take Inventory of Yourself

Vinay has a practical method for beginning, and it starts with honest self-assessment.

Understand what you are genuinely good at. Not what your job title says you do, but what you actually do well that other people cannot easily replicate. The ability to build trust with a specific type of client. The instinct that tells you when a situation is more complicated than it appears. The judgment that comes from having seen the same type of problem two dozen times and knowing which details matter.

Understand what you are not good at, or do not enjoy, or spend time on that frustrates you. Most people in knowledge work can identify, without much prompting, the part of their week that feels like overhead: the analysis that takes four hours because the data is always in the wrong format, the document that should take twenty minutes but always takes two hours because of the formatting, the research that is necessary but never interesting.

Use AI to fill the gaps. A strategic thinker whose written memos always read flat can use AI to draft the prose version of an argument they have already worked out, and then edit it against the judgment that produced the argument. A strong communicator who has never been confident with quantitative analysis can run models through AI and translate the output into language a client will actually absorb. An experienced advisor who dreads the quarterly review deck can let AI handle the visual layer so the presentation finally lands at the level of his thinking.

The Shift That Changes Everything

The shift from transactional to collaborative AI use is an individual one. It happens inside one person's mind. Here is how to know if you have made it: If you are using AI and it feels like a slightly faster version of your existing workflow, you are using it transactionally. If you are using AI and it feels like your mind has been connected to a power source you did not previously have access to, you have crossed into collaboration.

The difference is not about which tool you use or how often you use it. It is about whether the AI is changing how you think, not just what you produce.

Try this: Take the hardest strategic question on your desk right now, the one you have been deferring because you do not have a clean answer, and spend ninety minutes working through it with AI as a thinking partner. Not asking it to solve the problem. Asking it to help you think. Ask it what you might be missing. Ask it to argue the other side. Ask it what the data suggests. See what happens to your thinking.

Your Side of the Deal

The book argues for a mutual responsibility between organizations and the people who work in them. The organization's side is to invest in your development, tell you honestly what is changing, and be a partner in the transition rather than an administrator of it. Your side is to move.

The professional who is standing flat-footed when the technology arrives at their role is not a victim of the technology. They are a victim of the choice not to move when moving was still optional.

Moving does not mean mastering every AI tool. It means deciding, today, that the evolution of your work is a personal responsibility and not only an organizational one. It means spending time each week in genuine collaboration with AI on the actual hard work of your practice, not just the overhead. It means being willing to say, in your own head, that the way you have been doing some of your work may not be the way you will need to do it two years from now.

That sentence is the hardest sentence in this appendix. It is also the one that, if you sit with it honestly, opens the door to a version of your practice that is more focused, more effective, and more distinctly yours than the current one.

Three Things to Do This Week

1. Spend ninety minutes in genuine AI collaboration on your hardest current problem. Not for efficiency. For thinking.
2. Identify the three tasks in your work week that feel most like overhead and that AI could handle at least partially. Delegate one of them this week.
3. Ask yourself: What is the work that only I can do, that my clients or colleagues depend on me specifically to do? Write down three answers. That list is your practice. Protect it.

C

The Work Center Framework and Irreducibility Test

THE WORK CENTER is the unit of analysis where the WI Score's implications become operational. It is a coherent body of work inside the firm with defined inputs, defined outputs, and a measurable contribution to value. Most firms have between fifteen and one hundred of them. Universal examples include hiring a new employee, handling a customer support inquiry, and approving a vendor contract. Firm-specific examples in a benefits and consulting context include renewal benchmarking, fiduciary risk guidance, and cross-disciplinary client synthesis. The diagnostic in this appendix runs at the level of a single Work Center. Most of the configuration decisions that move the WI Score happen at this unit.

The Six Properties of Every Work Center

Inputs. The information that feeds the center. For a renewal benchmarking center: claims data, plan design, market benchmarks, regulatory parameters, the texture of the specific client relationship.

Processing. How judgment is actually rendered inside the center. Sometimes explicit, written down in a framework.

More often tacit, accumulated by a senior practitioner over years. The honest mapping always finds more tacit work than the practitioners themselves believed.

Outputs. The decisions, recommendations, and artifacts the rest of the firm depends on. Renewals delivered. Plans advised. Cases closed. Whatever this Work Center actually produces. This is also the unit that goes into the Output variable when the WI Score is calculated at the Work Center level.

Cadence. How often the center runs. High-cadence centers benefit from automation that scales without fatigue. Low-cadence, high-stakes centers benefit from depth of human preparation.

Stakes. What is at risk when the center fails. A misconfigured renewal benchmarking center produces a suboptimal recommendation that an advisor will catch in review. A misconfigured fiduciary risk guidance center produces legal exposure the client cannot recover from.

Ownership. Who is accountable when the center underperforms. Workforce Intelligence requires that every center have a named owner who is accountable for how it is configured, how it performs, and how it improves over time.

Intelligence and Capability

Every Work Center runs on two kinds of work. The first is cognitive work, the interpretation, judgment, and formation of the recommendation. The second is executional work, the drafting, formatting, calculation, and production of the artifact. The first is intelligence. The second is capability.

Intelligence and capability used to be bundled inside a single human because no other arrangement was possible. The advisor who formed the recommendation also drafted the memo. The underwriter who assessed the risk also produced the documentation. Org charts assumed bundling because the work could not be configured any other way. AI breaks the bundle. The two are now independently configurable, and the configuration becomes the strategic question. The most interesting moves are not at the level of the Work Center as a whole. They are at the level of the split inside the Work Center. Figure C.1 plots the two axes with examples of Work Centers across the map.

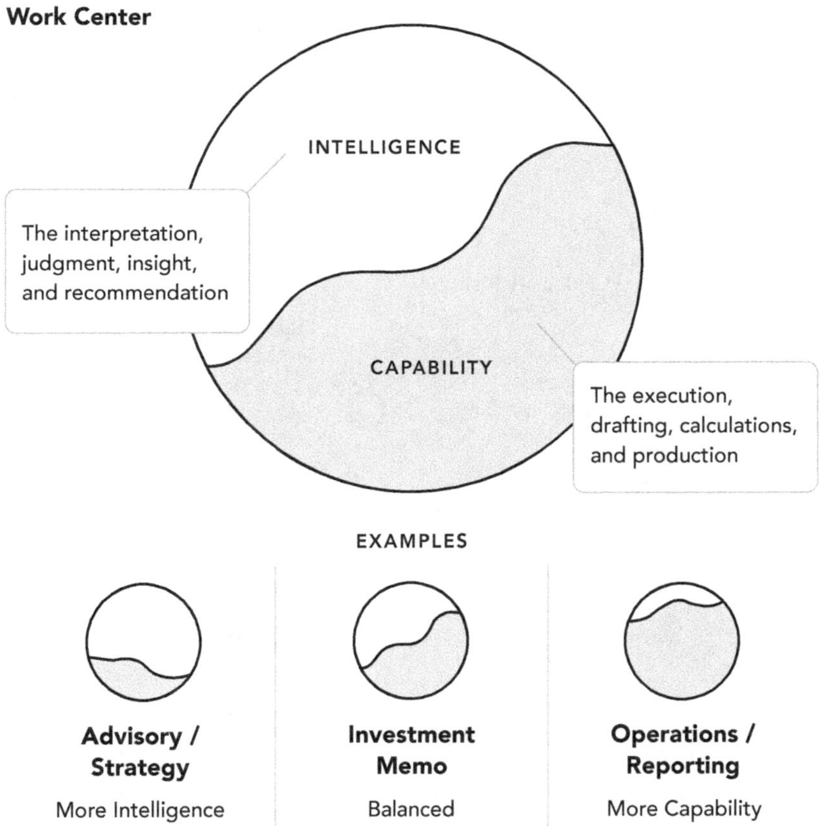

Figure C.1 The Intelligence–Capability map. Every Work Center can be plotted along two axes: Intelligence (the interpretation, judgment, insight, and recommendation required) and Capability (the execution, drafting, calculations, and production required). Examples shown—Advisory/Strategy, Investment Memo, and Operations/Reporting—illustrate placements ranging from more-intelligence to balanced to more-capability.

The Irreducibility Test below is therefore run on each side separately. The same Work Center can have irreducible intelligence and reducible capability, or partially irreducible intelligence with reducible capability, or both sides reducible. The configuration that fits each combination is different. Figure C.2 shows the four configurations the test produces.

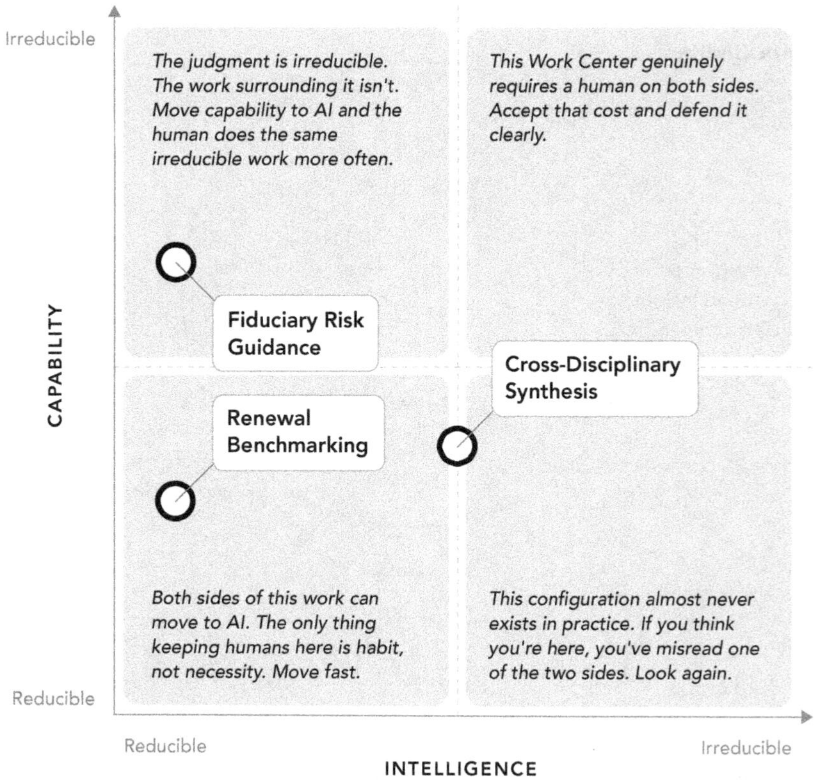

Figure C.2 The four configurations produced by applying the Irreducibility Test to both sides of a Work Center. The four cells reflect the combinations of irreducible and reducible intelligence and capability. Three of the four configurations occur in practice and are described in the accompanying text; the fourth (reducible intelligence with irreducible capability) almost never exists. Examples shown—Fiduciary Risk Guidance, Cross-Disciplinary Synthesis, and Renewal Benchmarking—are the three Work Centers used as worked examples in this appendix.

The Irreducibility Test

The test asks one question: Is the human judgment inside this Work Center structurally required, or is it residually present because the work was historically organized around human capability?

Structural conditions that produce irreducibility: Legal accountability that cannot be carried by an AI system. Trust relationships between professional and client that depend on the embodied presence of a human. Cross-disciplinary synthesis that requires integration of fields no single AI configuration spans. Situations that are genuinely novel in ways the model's training cannot anticipate. Stakes that require a level of accountability a system cannot bear.

Structural conditions that produce reducibility: Work that is data-driven and pattern-matching, where the answer is implicit in the data. Regulatory lookup, where the answer exists in publicly available sources. Comparison or benchmarking, where the analytic structure is repeatable across cases. Research synthesis, where the inputs are widely available and the synthesis is structured rather than novel.

Three Configuration Examples

The three examples below illustrate the diagnostic running on real Work Centers inside OneDigital and producing three different configuration outcomes.

Example One: Renewal Benchmarking. This Work Center compares a client's current benefits plan against market benchmarks at renewal, identifies optimization opportunities, and produces a recommendation for an advisor to take into the renewal conversation. Inputs include claims data, plan design, market benchmarks, and the texture of the client relationship. Output is renewals delivered. Cadence is high, hundreds of runs per week. Stakes are moderate; an advisor catches suboptimal recommendations in review.

Apply the Irreducibility Test on each side. The intelligence runs on pattern matching against a large dataset of comparable plans and is reducible. The capability is also reducible. Both sides move to AI.

The configuration moves intelligence and capability to AI. The model produces the benchmarking analysis and the optimization recommendation. The advisor reviews the output, applies client-specific context the configuration could not account for, and signs off. The first benefit is throughput. The second benefit, less expected, is consistency. Under the old configuration, the quality of any single benchmarking depended on which advisor pulled the analysis and how much time the advisor had that week. The new configuration produces uniform depth across all renewals in the queue.

Example Two: Fiduciary Risk Guidance. This Work Center counsels a client on the obligations that come with sponsoring a benefits plan, identifies exposures, and recommends mitigation. Inputs include plan documents, regulatory parameters, the client's posture, and continuing case law. Output is plans advised. Cadence is moderate. Stakes are high; the firm and the client both carry legal exposure for the recommendation.

Apply the Irreducibility Test. The intelligence is irreducible. No current AI system can carry the legal accountability or render the contextual judgment the recommendation requires. The capability is reducible.

The configuration keeps the intelligence with the senior advisor and moves the capability work to AI. Once the advisor renders the judgment, the model produces documentation, the client memo, meeting preparation, follow-up communications, and the internal compliance record. The senior advisor who used to run two of these in a week now runs four. The executional layer around the judgment had been consuming the time. Removing it freed the judgment to happen more often.

Example Three: Cross-Disciplinary Client Synthesis. This Work Center pulls benefits, retirement, HR consulting, and tax planning into a single integrated recommendation for a client that requires an integrated view. Inputs come from multiple specialist disciplines. Output is integrated recommendations delivered. Cadence is low. Stakes are high.

Apply the Irreducibility Test. The intelligence has two parts. Assembly of specialized inputs from each discipline is reducible; AI can pull faster and more comprehensively than any single senior consultant. The synthesis itself, the holding of multiple domains in view simultaneously to produce an integrated result, is irreducible. The capability work that follows the synthesis is reducible.

The configuration reflects the split. AI assembles the inputs. The senior consultant synthesizes. AI then produces the capability outputs that follow the synthesis. Cross-disciplinary capacity expanded for clients that had been beyond the reach of any single consultant's time. The quality of the synthesis stayed where it needed to be.

None of the three configurations would have been visible from a single high-level question along the lines of "should we use AI for this Work Center?" All three became visible when the diagnostic was applied to the intelligence and capability sides separately and the bundle inside each Work Center was honestly mapped.

The Four Questions for Monday Morning

First: Is your AI Amplification Factor (Variable A) rising, and where is it weakest? A flat or low A across the firm is the constraint the rest of the analysis has to address. Locate the parts of the firm where A is dragging.

Second: Which Work Centers are most responsible for your firm-wide A? A weak A is not evenly distributed. Identify the top ten Work Centers contributing to your constraint. For each one, name the owner. For each one, calculate A within the Work Center using the same survey question applied to its participants.

Third: Inside each of those Work Centers, what is the bundle that has not been broken? Where is intelligence and capability still bundled inside a single human, not because the bundling produces the best outcome, but because the work has always been organized that way? Run the Irreducibility Test on the intelligence side and on the capability side separately.

Fourth: Who in your firm is accountable for the configuration of your Work Centers, considered as a portfolio rather than as isolated functions? If the answer is no one specifically, you are operating without the discipline this framework describes.

D

The Coworker Job Description Template and Opportunity Scorecard

THE JOB DESCRIPTION is written before any technology decision is made. It is the document that makes a Coworker deployment a talent decision rather than a software purchase.

The Six Elements of Every Coworker Job Description

1. **Knowledge Domain.** What does this Coworker know? List the specific documents, data sources, regulatory and market references, and organizational materials you consider authoritative. Describe the standard of knowledge to which you would hold a new senior hire. This is also the Coworker's continuing education curriculum: When the market changes, this is what gets updated.
2. **Primary Responsibilities.** The three to five core functions this Coworker performs, stated specifically and tied to outcomes the business cares about. A software specification would say assists with research. A job description says: prepares client situation summaries ahead of advisory meetings, identifying key renewal risk factors, relevant benchmark comparisons, and the strategic questions the advisor should be prepared to address.

3. **Working Relationships.** Who does this Coworker serve? Who interacts with it daily? Which other Coworkers does it work alongside? Making these relationships explicit produces management discipline that informal understanding never does.
4. **Performance Expectations.** What does success look like at thirty days, at ninety days, at one year? Who is responsible for the evaluation? If the honest answer to what does success look like is we will figure that out later, the deployment is not ready to begin.
5. **Scope Boundaries.** What this Coworker will not do, stated explicitly. The boundaries serve a governance function and an adoption function: They set accurate expectations so that users' first experience falls within the Coworker's capability rather than at its edges.
6. **Designated Supervisor.** The named human owner. Non-negotiable. The Supervisor must be identified before the build begins, not after deployment. The Supervisor is the human who curates the Coworker's intelligence, monitors its performance, updates its knowledge base, reviews user feedback, and decides what to improve.

The Seven-Dimension Opportunity Scorecard

Score each dimension from 1 to 3. A total of 18 to 21 is a strong candidate for a first deployment. Below 12, reconsider or defer.

Volume (1–3): How frequently does this work occur? Daily or more: 3. Weekly: 2. Monthly or less: 1.

Knowledge availability (1–3): Is the required expertise documented and accessible? Fully documented: 3. Partially documented: 2. Primarily tacit: 1.

Output measurability (1–3): Can a domain expert determine whether the Coworker's output is correct or incorrect? Clearly verifiable: 3. Somewhat verifiable: 2. Largely subjective: 1.

Time burden (1–3): Do the people currently performing this work feel frustrated by the hours it requires? Strong felt burden: 3. Moderate burden: 2. Minimal burden: 1.

Supervisor availability (1–3): Does a natural Supervisor exist, someone who feels the pain this Coworker is designed to solve and has the expertise to curate it? Identified and motivated: 3. Possible candidate: 2. No clear candidate: 1.

User readiness (1–3): Is the user population ready and willing to engage? Enthusiastic early adopters present: 3. Neutral: 2. Resistant: 1.

Strategic alignment (1–3): Does this Coworker address a high-priority business need? Core to strategy: 3. Adjacent: 2. Nice-to-have: 1.

E

The Hybrid Workforce Architecture

THE HYBRID WORKFORCE is not a program to be completed. It is an organizational capability to be developed, and like all capabilities, it grows stronger through use. This appendix summarizes the five-tier human fluency model and the three types of AI that make up the full hybrid workforce.

The Five Tiers of Human Fluency

Tier One: The AI User. Every employee. Required ninety-minute hands-on workshop before access is granted. Not a webinar about features. A session where people work with their actual Coworker on real scenarios from their practice. Completion of this workshop is a baseline of employment, not a checkbox.

Tier Two: The Manager. Every people manager. Required half-day workshop before their team's Coworker deployment. Six adoption behaviors: use tools daily, share what you are learning, make AI fluency your personal KPI, run the demo personally, protect learning time, bring AI into client interactions.

Tier Three: The Coworker Supervisor. Named owner of a specific Coworker. Responsible for knowledge base curation, use case development, adoption work, and formal performance reviews. Should be your best senior practitioner in the relevant domain. Bi-weekly one-on-ones with the Coworker. Monthly feedback review. Quarterly deep review.

Tier Four: The AI Fellow. Super users and adoption champions. Demonstrate what good engagement with a Coworker looks like. Pull colleagues forward. Responsible for surfacing prompts, workflows, and refinements that compound across the practice.

Tier Five: The Builder. Domain practitioners who have crossed the threshold of being able to ship working technology using AI development tools. Not engineers. People from inside the business who understand what needs to be built because they do the work. Supported by the central AI and product team for architecture, security, and production deployment.

Three Types of AI in the Hybrid Workforce

Coworkers assist with cognition: research, analysis, drafting, summarizing, synthesizing. Ben, Dex, Nina, Amy, Quinn, Avery, Jackie, Odysseus, Charity, and Ace are Coworkers. They handle thinking work alongside a human practitioner who directs, reviews, and applies judgment the Coworker cannot.

Agents are autonomous: They perceive changes through data and act on behalf of the team without being prompted in the moment. The accuracy threshold for agentic capabilities is much higher than for cognitive Coworkers, and the governance is correspondingly stricter.

Builders are the human-driven, AI-built technology surfaces the firm uses to run, sell, and deliver. The applications, dashboards, client deliverables, and intelligent workflows that an AI practitioner from inside the business ships using AI development tools.

F

The Intelligence Map Starter Guide

The intelligence map is a practice, not a document. Its purpose is to give every workforce decision an anchor. This guide is the starting point for organizations beginning the exercise.

What You Need

A workforce census stripped of names and contact information: job titles and salary bands, keyed to the company's business. Two hours with the person in your firm who understands how work actually flows, who is almost never the person whose title suggests they should be. A willingness to ask honestly where the intelligence of your firm lives today, and where you want it to live in eighteen months.

The Two-Hour Leadership Session Agenda

First thirty minutes: Map the roles. For each role represented on the census, ask: Where does the intelligence of this role live? Is it in documents, in heads, in processes, in client relationships, or some combination? How documented is it? How transferable is it if the person leaves?

Second thirty minutes: Identify the gaps. Which parts of which roles are being performed by humans not because the humans are the right vessel for the work, but because no one has built the alternative? Which tasks are the most experienced people spending time on that AI could now handle? Which client problems are going unsolved because the firm does not have the bandwidth?

Third thirty minutes: Identify the opportunities. For each gap identified, ask: What would change in how the firm serves its clients if this gap were closed? Which gaps, if addressed by an AI Coworker, would most immediately improve the quality and reach of the firm's work?

Final thirty minutes: Name the first Coworker. Based on the exercise, identify the single highest-scoring opportunity against the seven-dimension scorecard in Appendix D. Name the Supervisor. Agree on a timeline for the job description.

The Quarterly Refresh

At the end of each quarter, return to the intelligence map with three questions. First: What has changed in the technology landscape that changes where intelligence should sit? Second: What did our Coworker deployments teach us about where intelligence actually lives versus where we assumed it lived? Third: Where is the next highest-value gap to address?

The map is a tool for navigating a technology environment that changes too quickly for any static plan to survive. The discipline of returning to it quarterly is what separates firms that compound their advantage from firms that make a few good decisions and plateau.

G

Monday Morning Checklist

One action from each chapter. Ninety days to activation.

WEEK 1–2 | From the Introduction

Name your fear honestly. Write down the specific question about AI and your organization that you have been avoiding. The question you keep thinking about but have not said out loud in a leadership meeting. That is where the work starts.

WEEK 1–2 | From Chapter 1

Build or find your red dot. If you have not yet run a disruption assessment for your organization, do it this week. Use one of the publicly available AI readiness tools, or adapt the methodology from Chapter 1. Get a number. Look at it.

WEEK 2–3 | From Chapter 2

Map your Coworkers. Walk through your organization and list every AI tool, workflow, or system that is currently doing work that used to require a person. Name each one. Assign an owner. If you cannot name an owner, that is the first gap to close.

WEEK 3–4 | From Chapter 3

Calculate your WI Score. Run the three conversations in Appendix A. Get a number. Place it on the band table. Identify the one variable that is dragging your score down most.

WEEK 4–5 | From Chapter 4

Have your collaborative AI session. Spend ninety minutes working through your hardest current strategic question with AI as a thinking partner, not an answer machine. If it feels like a slightly faster version of your existing workflow, you are still transactional. Keep going.

WEEK 5–6 | From Chapter 5

Name your Avery. Identify the leader in your organization who most resembles Avery: urgency, no framework, waiting to be shown how. Have the conversation. Give them the language.

WEEK 6–7 | From Chapter 6

Write one job description. Pick the highest-scoring opportunity from the Appendix D scorecard. Write the job description for that Coworker before you make any technology decision. Name the Supervisor. This takes one day.

WEEK 7–8 | From Chapter 7

Start the Internship. Begin building your first Coworker. Set up the Internship cohort of five to ten users. Run the first iteration cycle. Do not launch to the full population until the Supervisor has signed off on the output quality.

WEEK 8–10 | From Chapter 8

Run the Tier Two workshop. Before your first Coworker reaches the Apprenticeship, run the half-day manager workshop with every people manager in the affected practice. The adoption numbers live here.

WEEK 10–12 | From Chapter 9

Have the honest conversation. In your next leadership team meeting, say plainly: The identity question is real, the transition is hard, and we are going to address it directly. Name one person whose transition you are personally going to invest in.

WEEK 10–12 | From Chapter 10

Start the intelligence map. Run the two-hour session from Appendix F. Get a first-draft map. Set a quarterly refresh date.

ONGOING | From Chapter 11

Keep the deal. Every quarter, ask: Are we holding up our side of the mutual responsibility? Are we investing in development before we have to? Are we telling our people honestly what is changing? The deal has to be renewed. It does not sustain itself.

The workforce is no longer just human. Managing it as if it were is a choice that becomes more expensive every quarter.

NOW MOVE.

Notes

Chapter 1

1. Ethan Mollick, *Co-Intelligence: Living and Working with AI* (New York: Portfolio/Penguin, 2024). https://www.penguinrandomhouse.com/books/741805/co-intelligence-by-ethan-mollick/.
2. Mollick surveys multiple studies suggesting productivity gains of 20 to 80 percent across knowledge-work categories. See Mollick, *Co-Intelligence*, chapters 4–5.

Chapter 2

1. Gallup, *State of the Global Workplace: 2024 Report* (Washington, DC: Gallup, 2024), https://www.gallup.com/workplace/349484/state-of-the-global-workplace.aspx.
2. Ravin Jesuthasan and Tanuj Kapilashrami, *The Skills-Powered Organization: The Journey to the Next-Generation Enterprise* (Cambridge, MA: MIT Press, 2024).

Chapter 3

1. Microsoft, "2025: The Year the Frontier Firm Is Born," 2025 Annual Work Trend Index Report, April 23, 2025. https://www.microsoft.com/en-us/worklab/work-trend-index/2025-the-year-the-frontier-firm-is-born.
2. Robert S. Kaplan and David P. Norton, "The Balanced Scorecard: Measures That Drive Performance," *Harvard Business Review* 70, no. 1 (January–February 1992): 71–79. https://hbr.org/1992/01/the-balanced-scorecard-measures-that-drive-performance-2.
3. Robert M. Solow, "Technical Change and the Aggregate Production Function," *Review of Economics and Statistics* 39, no. 3 (August 1957): 312–320. https://doi.org/10.2307/1926047.
4. Erik Brynjolfsson, Daniel Rock, and Chad Syverson, "The Productivity J-Curve: How Intangibles Complement General Purpose Technologies," *American Economic Journal: Macroeconomics* 13, no. 1 (January 2021): 333–372. https://doi.org/10.1257/mac.20180386.

Chapter 4

1. Microsoft, "2025: The Year the Frontier Firm Is Born," 2025 Annual Work Trend Index Report, April 23, 2025. The survey of 31,000 knowledge workers across 31 countries was conducted by Edelman Data x Intelligence between February 6 and March 24, 2025. https://www.microsoft.com/en-us/worklab/work-trend-index/2025-the-year-the-frontier-firm-is-born.
2. David Heinemeier Hansson, interview by Gergely Orosz, "DHH's New Way of Writing Code," *The Pragmatic Engineer Podcast*, April 8, 2026. https://newsletter.pragmaticengineer.com/p/dhhs-new-way-of-writing-code.
3. Zapier, "Raising the AI Fluency Bar for Every Zapier Hire," Zapier Blog, March 31, 2026. https://zapier.com/blog/raising-ai-fluency-bar-in-hiring/. The post cites as its empirical anchor Anthropic, "Anthropic Education Report: The AI Fluency Index," February 23, 2026. https://www.anthropic.com/research/AI-fluency-index.

Chapter 5

1. Microsoft and LinkedIn, "2024 Work Trend Index Annual Report," May 2024. The survey covered knowledge workers across 31 markets and found that 75 percent of knowledge workers were using AI at work, with 78 percent bringing their own tools (BYOAI). https://blogs.microsoft.com/blog/2024/05/08/microsoft-and-linkedin-release-the-2024-work-trend-index-on-the-state-of-ai-at-work/.
2. Gartner, "Copilot for Microsoft 365: Assessing the Impact and Value So Far," August 2024. The survey found 60 percent of respondents were running pilots, with 48 percent planning small-scale deployments. Only 6 percent had finished their pilot and were moving to large-scale deployment. https://www.gartner.com/en/documents/5659223.
3. Reporting on the 2025 Gartner Microsoft 365 and Copilot Survey, presented at a Gartner conference, found 5 percent of organizations that had finished pilots were moving to larger deployment. The analyst quoted is Matt Wilson, Gartner VP Analyst. See "Gartner: Microsoft Copilot Hype Offset by ROI and Readiness Realities," TechPartner News, June 26, 2025. https://www.techpartner.news/news/gartner-microsoft-copilot-hype-offset-by-roi-and-readiness-realities-618118.
4. "Microsoft Copilot Adoption: From Enterprise Rollout to Habitual Usage," Whatfix Blog, January 2026. The analysis attributed low adoption to organizations treating AI deployment as a standard software rollout rather than a behavior change initiative. https://whatfix.com/blog/microsoft-copilot-adoption/.
5. Josh Bersin, "The Pivotal Role of Chief HR Officer in AI Transformation," Josh Bersin (blog), October 10, 2025. Bersin identifies multiple companies where the CHRO or CPO has taken a leading role in enterprise AI adoption, including Microsoft, Moderna, and HubSpot. https://joshbersin.com/2025/10/the-pivotal-role-of-chief-hr-officer-in-ai-transformation/.

Chapter 6

1. Ravin Jesuthasan and John W. Boudreau, *Reinventing Jobs: A 4-Step Approach for Applying Automation to Work* (Boston: Harvard Business Review Press, 2018); Ravin Jesuthasan and Tanuj Kapilashrami, *The Skills-Powered Organization: The Journey to the Next-Generation Enterprise* (Cambridge, MA: MIT Press, 2024).

Chapter 8

1. Paul Graham, "Founder Mode," Paul Graham (blog), September 2024. Graham's essay drew on a talk Brian Chesky delivered at a Y Combinator event the same month. https://paulgraham.com/foundermode.html
2. Society for Human Resource Management, *From Adoption to Empowerment: Shaping the AI-Driven Workforce of Tomorrow* (Alexandria, VA: SHRM, July 2025). The report surveyed 1,812 U.S.-based workers in January 2025. Among workers who rated their organization's AI and human-intelligence integration as excellent, 97 percent reported satisfaction with available training. Among those rating integration as fair or poor, the figures were 21 percent and 18 percent respectively. https://urldefense.com/v3/__https://www.shrm.org/topics-tools/research/from-adoption-to-empowerment--shaping-the-ai-driven-workforce-of-tomorrow__;!!N11eV2iwtfs!tZVAMZe3SJTOZI8QAe-x7XTcDU5ZhCy70Z1SgXiV2mForJ4NXg6GA_5QUnfurOCeWST5ak6XhchSM8hxa26uK2KW9Q$

Chapter 9

1. Center for Humane Technology, "The CHT Perspective," Center for Humane Technology, accessed April 2026. https://www.humanetech.com/the-cht-perspective. See also Damon Isherwood, "The Center for Humane Technology: Fighting the Human Downgrade," *The Times of Israel*, November 15, 2024. https://blogs.timesofisrael.com/the-center-for-humane-technology-fighting-the-human-downgrade/

2. Center for Humane Technology, "Home," Center for Humane Technology, accessed April 2026. "CHT is currently supporting trailblazing litigation that spotlights the dangers of anthropomorphic design in AI chatbots." https://www.humanetech.com/
3. Karen Shanley, "General AI Will Be World-Ending If We Don't Stop It Now," Karen Shanley (blog), April 2026. Harris's stated policy recommendations include the direct instruction to "Ban or limit anthropomorphizing AI to prevent emotional attachment." https://karenshanley.com/general-ai-will-be-world-ending-if-we-dont-stop-it-now/
4. Authors' summary of Sandra Peter, Kai Riemer and Jevin D. West et al., "The Benefits and Dangers of Anthropomorphic Conversational Agents," *Proceedings of the National Academy of Sciences* 122 (2025). https://www.pnas.org/doi/10.1073/pnas.2415898122
5. Eileen Roesler, Dietrich Manzey, and Linda Onnasch, "A Meta-Analysis on the Effectiveness of Anthropomorphism in Human-Robot Interaction," *Science Robotics* 6, no. 58 (2021). Summary reported in Andrea Thomas and Mirjam Boch, "To Trust or Not to Trust a Human(-Like) AI," *Zeitschrift für Arbeitswissenschaft*, September 2025. https://www.science.org/doi/10.1126/scirobotics.abj5425
6. Brenda Leong and Evan Selinger, "Robot Eyes Wide Shut: Understanding Dishonest Anthropomorphism," *Proceedings of the 2019 ACM Conference on Fairness, Accountability, and Transparency* (FAT* '19), 2019. For applied commentary, see David L. Hudson Jr., "The Danger of Dishonest Anthropomorphism in Chatbot Design," *Psychology Today*, January 8, 2024. https://www.psychologytoday.com/us/blog/virtue-in-the-media-world/202401/the-danger-of-dishonest-anthropomorphism-in-chatbot-design
7. Arman Shehabi et al., 2024 United States Data Center Energy Usage Report, LBNL-2001637 (Berkeley, CA: Lawrence Berkeley National Laboratory, December 2024). https://eta-publications.lbl.gov/sites/default/files/2024-12/lbnl-2024-united-states-data-center-energy-usage-report_1.pdf. See also U.S. Department of Energy, "DOE Releases New Report Evaluating Increase in Electricity Demand from Data Centers," December 4, 2024. https://www.energy.gov/articles/doe-releases-new-report-evaluating-increase-electricity-demand-data-centers.

8. "Data Center Energy Consumption Forecast, 2024–2030," ABI Research, accessed May 2026, https://www.abiresearch.com/blog/data-center-energy-consumption-forecast (reporting cooling at 37 percent of data center power). See also "How Much Electricity Does a Data Center Use? Complete 2025 Analysis," IAEI Magazine, January 2026. https://iaeimagazine.org/electrical-fundamentals/how-much-electricity-does-a-data-center-use-complete-2025-analysis/.
9. Shehabi et al., 2024 United States Data Center Energy Usage Report; figures summarized in Lawrence Susskind, Caroline Hill, and Yasmin Zaerpoor, "Data Centers Consume Massive Amounts of Water," The Conversation, August 19, 2025. https://theconversation.com/data-centers-consume-massive-amounts-of-water-companies-rarely-tell-the-public-exactly-how-much-262901.
10. "Data Centres and Water: Understanding the Real Impact," STL Partners, March 25, 2026. https://stlpartners.com/articles/data-centres/data-centres-and-water/. See also "Myths vs. Reality: Data Centers and Water Usage," Florida Water and Pollution Control Operators Association, accessed May 2026. https://www.fwpcoa.org/content.aspx?page_id=5&club_id=859275&item_id=130961.
11. Sebastian Moss, "Starcloud-1 satellite reaches space, with Nvidia H100 GPU now operating in orbit," Data Center Dynamics, November 4, 2025. https://www.datacenterdynamics.com/en/news/starcloud-1-satellite-reaches-space-with-nvidia-h100-gpu-now-operating-in-orbit/.
12. Philip Johnston quoted in Tereza Pultarova, "NVIDIA's H100 GPU Takes Data Centers to Space," IEEE Spectrum, November 4, 2025. https://spectrum.ieee.org/nvidia-h100-space. See also Aria Alamalhodaei, "Starcloud raises $170 million Series A to build data centers in space," TechCrunch, March 30, 2026. https://techcrunch.com/2026/03/30/starcloud-raises-170-million-series-ato-build-data-centers-in-space/.
13. Calum Chace, "Data Centers in Space: Will 2027 Really Be the Year AI Goes to Orbit?" Singularity Hub, December 19, 2025. https://singularityhub.com/2025/12/19/data-centers-in-space-will-2027-really-be-the-year-ai-goes-to-orbit/.

14. Beals et al., "Exploring a space-based, scalable AI infrastructure system design." See also "The 'Physics Wall': Orbiting Data Centers Face a Massive Cooling Challenge," SatNews, March 17, 2026. https://satnews.com/2026/03/17/the-physics-wall-orbiting-data-centers-face-a-massive-cooling-challenge/.

Chapter 10

1. Cassidy is one of several enterprise AI agent platforms that allow organizations to build and deploy AI Coworkers across multiple large language model providers, including Anthropic, OpenAI, and Google. Similar platform approaches have emerged from vendors including LangChain, CrewAI, and Microsoft Copilot Studio. See Cassidy AI, "Product Overview," Cassidy, accessed April 2026. https://www.cassidyai.com/.
2. The OneDigital workforce assessment tool draws on several widely cited sources on AI's impact on work, including the World Economic Forum's *Future of Jobs Report 2025*, which surveyed employers representing more than 14 million workers across 55 economies, and McKinsey Global Institute's research on generative AI and the future of work, which analyzed occupational exposure across more than 800 job categories. See World Economic Forum, *The Future of Jobs Report 2025* (Geneva: World Economic Forum, January 2025). https://www.weforum.org/publications/the-future-of-jobs-report-2025/. See also McKinsey Global Institute, "Generative AI and the Future of Work in America," McKinsey & Company, July 2023. https://www.mckinsey.com/mgi/our-research/generative-ai-and-the-future-of-work-in-america.

Acknowledgments

TO OUR FAMILIES: Thank you for the patience that does not show up in any chapter and the steadiness that shows up in every one. The early mornings, the late nights, the weekends lost to this manuscript and the ones lost to the work the manuscript is about, none of this happens without you.

To the 6,000+ colleagues who make up OneDigital: This is your book as much as it is ours. The Workforce Intelligence framework was built inside a live business, by people who chose to run toward the unknown. You let us experiment. You pushed back when we got it wrong. You kept serving our clients while we figured out what came next. Every page in this book carries your fingerprints.

To Adam Bruckman, our co-founder and CEO, and to the leadership team and Board of OneDigital: Thank you for the conviction to invest in this work before it was obvious, and for the trust to let us share what we learned.

About the Authors

Mike Sullivan

Mike Sullivan has spent more than four decades at the intersection of business strategy, mergers and acquisitions, and all facets of an evolving American workplace and has seen firsthand what separates companies that thrive from those that stall. As Co-Founder and Chief Growth Officer of OneDigital, he has helped build one of the most dynamic insurance and financial services firms in the country, guiding its expansion through acquisition, partnership, and entry into new markets. Outside OneDigital, he is an active investor and board member across a broad set of firms and industry verticals.

Mike holds a bachelor's degree in history from Amherst College and an MBA from George Mason University, with international coursework at Oxford University. He lives in Virginia with his wife, Patti, and has three grown children.

Vinay Gidwaney

As Chief Product Officer (CPO), Vinay Gidwaney is passionate about applying AI and emerging technologies to help employees and families make better decisions around their finances and benefits through OneDigital's integrated offerings. He leads a strong team of technology experts, AI engineers, and product developers building the next generation of intelligent solutions for OneDigital's customer base. A seasoned technologist and entrepreneur working at the intersection of AI, insurance, and product innovation, Vinay began his career as co-founder of Control-F1, a pioneer in remote IT management software, which was acquired by Computer Associates (CA). During this period, he was named to MIT Technology Review's TR35, recognizing him as one of the world's top innovators under the age of thirty-five, an honor he received at age twenty, making him one of the youngest recipients in the program's history. He later served as a Visiting Researcher with the Synthetic Neurobiology group at the MIT Media Lab, where he explored the frontiers of intelligence and brain-computer interfaces.

Vinay went on to found Maxwell Health, where he pioneered a new model for employee benefits and grew the company to serve thousands of customers before its acquisition by Sun Life Financial. In response to the global COVID-19 pandemic, he served as Head of Technology at Boston-based CIC Health, leveraging innovative technology to help stand up and scale one of the largest mass vaccination efforts in the country across Massachusetts. In addition to his role at OneDigital, Vinay is a Board Member at the education and social justice nonprofit Design for Change USA and sits on the advisory boards of several startups across the AI, insurtech, life sciences, and healthcare industries. He lives in Brookline, Massachusetts, with his wife and four children.

Index

A

Accountability, 56–57
Affordable Care Act (ACA), xiii, xiv
AI, *see* Artificial intelligence
AI Agents, 120
AI Amplification Factor (variable A):
  adding, to surveys, 180–191
  development of, 36–38
  hiring for upper bands of, 56
  psychological shift needed to raise, 45
AI Builders, 120
AI Coworkers:
  benefits of, 66–68
  defining, 120
  emotions about, 133
  finding right problem for first deployment, 82
  human coworkers needed for, 169
  and intelligence mapping, 159–160
  observability of, 155–156
  as team members, 103, 136–137
  treated as human talent, 66, 67
AI fluency, as KPI, 114
AI Fluency Rubric, 55–57
AI hiring process, 93–104
  Apprenticeship phase, 96–98
  firing AI, 98–99
  Full-Time phase, 99–101
  Internship phase, 94–96
  and ongoing Supervisor education, 101–104
AI-native solutions, 136, 172
Airbnb, 109
AI transformation, 3–16
  concerns about, 143–147
  differing perspectives of, 174
  fear about, xv, 12–14
  humanity test in, 168–170
  as human-led, 9–12, 65–70
  and J-Curve, 40
  lack of alternatives to, 143–144
  new framework for, 14–16
  overcoming resistance to, 139–140
  realization of need for, 3–9
  as talent management, 33
  treating as an event, 124–125
  treating as IT project, 63–65
AI User (Tier One training), 112–113, 199
Altman, Sam, 151
American Economic Journal: Macroeconomics, 39
Anthropic, 56
Apprenticeship phase, 93, 96–98
Architecture:
  for AI talent, 153–154
  for hybrid workforce, 199–200

Artificial intelligence (AI):
- addressing assumptions about, 143–147
- as disruption, xiii–xiv
- employees' views of, 34–35
- employing specialists vs. general AI, 86–89
- environmental concerns about, 145–146
- fear related to, xi–xiii
- to fill gaps in personal skills, 185
- giving employees greater capabilities, 117–118
- lack of management system for, 22–23
- perspectives about AI use, 167–168
- sorting tasks for AI alone or collaboration, 79–81
- as talent in organizations, 15
- types of, in hybrid workforce, 119–124, 200
- using other company's, 155
- working with people, instead of replacing people, 10–12

Assessment tools, for intelligence mapping, 158
Authenticity concern, 47–50, 56–57

B

Bands, of WI scores, 40–41, 57
Baseball scouting, 23–24
Beane, Billy, 23
Behavioral shifts, measuring, 34–39
Ben (AI Coworker):
- development of, 75–79
- in Full-Time phase, 100
- in Internship phase, 95
- ongoing education for, 101–103, 115
- writing job description for, 82

Bersin, Josh, 65
BlackRock Infrastructure Summit, 151
Breaking Benefit Barriers, 86, 101, 115
"Bring Your Own AI" (BYOAI), 63
Bruckman, Adam, xvi, 11–13
Brynjolfsson, Erik, 39
Builders:
- as fifth tier in AI fluency training, 117–119, 200
- roles of, 108

Bukowski, Stan, 52–54, 114
BYOAI ("Bring Your Own AI"), 63

C

Cadence:
- of ongoing education, 124–125
- in Work Centers, 188

Capability, 188–189
Carew, Bill, 140, 142
Carew, John, 47–49, 116–117
Cassidy, 155
Center for Humane Technology (CHT), 133
Centralization, 108, 127
Chesky, Brian, 109
Chief Financial Officer (CFO), 179–180
Chief Human Resources Officer (CHRO), 21
Chief People Officer (CPO), 21
- AI transformation led by, 15
- intelligence mapping by, 159
- perspective of, in choosing solutions, 27–28
- as responsible for AI transformation, 65–66
- Workforce Intelligence scores used by, 29

Chrane, Elizabeth, 19, 28, 113, 139
CHRO (Chief Human Resources Officer), 21
CHT (Center for Humane Technology), 133
Claude, 4
Claude Opus 4.7, 135
Client interactions, bringing AI into, 114
Coaching, by AI Coworkers, 78
Cohorts, through three-phase lifecycle, 96
Co-intelligence, 45
Co-Intelligence (Mollick), 9
Collaborative AI use, 45–57
- with 3 types of AI, 121–124
- and authenticity concern, 47–50
- by employees, 34–35
- examples of, 45
- and Irreducibility Test, 190–193
- at OneDigital, 50–55
- productivity gains with, 9
- shifting to, 185
- at Zapier, 55–57

Command-based tools, AI as, 34–35
Communicating, with AI, 135–136
Compensation, for Supervisors, 86

Compounding:
- with collaborative AI use, 48
- in Full-Time phase, 100
- in hybrid workforce, 126–128
- and ownership of intelligence, 161–163
- to recoup time investment in AI Coworkers, 115

Consumer interfaces, for AI, 156
Copilot, 64, 65
Coworker Supervisor (Tier Three training), 114–115, 199–200
CPO, *see* Chief People Officer
Create (AI sorting mechanism), 80, 81
Customer relationship management software, 152

D

Data centers, 145–146
Data independence, 152
Developing firms, 40–41
Digital Workplace survey, 64
Disruptions:
- and humanity test, 169
- surviving, xiii–xiv

Dot-com collapse, xiii, xiv

E

Education, ongoing:
- for AI Coworkers, 86
- for hybrid workforce, 124–125
- for Supervisors, 101–104

Eliminate (AI sorting mechanism), 79, 81
Emotions, related to AI Coworkers, 133
Employees:
- ahead of leaders, in AI transformation, 13–14
- behavioral shifts in, 57
- engagement of, 21
- given a stake in training AI Coworkers, 97
- perceiving value of, 5–6
- personal responsibilities of, 173, 185–186
- personal WI playbook for, 183–186

Enterprise AI collaboration, 61–70
- difficulties integrating, 61–66
- as HR responsibility, 66–69

Enterprise intelligence mapping, 158
Environmental concerns about AI, 145–146

F

Failures, documenting, 162–163
Falk, Keith, 19, 20, 23–24
Fear:
- about AI transformation, xv, 12–14, 173
- about being replaced by AI, 51, 85, 138–144
- related to AI, xi–xiii
- trying to respond to, 183–184

Feedback:
- in Apprenticeship phase, 96–97
- in Full-time phase, 100

Fellows:
- as fourth tier in AI fluency training, 115–117, 200
- roles of, 108

Fellowship program, 108
Fernando, Randima, 133
Firing AI, 98–99
Five-tier fluency model, 199–200
- and compounding, 126–127
- for hybrid workforce, 111–119

Founder Mode, 109–110, 128
From Adoption to Empowerment (Society for Human Resource Management), 111
Full-Time phase, 93, 99–101

G

Gallup, 21
Gartner, 64
Global pandemic, xiii–xiv
Graham, Paul, 109

H

Hansson, David Heinemeier, 50
Harris, Tristan, 133, 137
Harvard Business Review, 36
HCM, *see* Human Capital Management
Her (film), 137
HR departments:
- AI transformation led by, 15, 65–69
- discussing WI scores with, 180–181

HRIS (Human Resource Information System), 28
HubSpot, 65
Human Capital Management (HCM), 14–16, 20–22, 24, 27

Human intelligence,
irreducibility of, 29–30
Humanity test, xv–xvi, 167–176
in AI transformation, 168–170
and hybrid workforce, 171–174
and irreducibility, 170–171
and perspectives about AI use, 167–168
Humanization of AI, 131–147
addressing assumptions about AI, 143–147
arguments for and against, 131–136
and value of individuals, 138–143
in work vs. personal contexts, 136–138
Human-led AI transformation, 9–12
Human Resource Information System (HRIS), 28
Hybrid workforce, 107–128
architecture for, 199–200
compounding in, 126–128
five-tier fluency model for, 111–119, 199–200
and Founder Mode, 109–110
and humanity test, 171–174
importance of training people in, 110–111
managing, with Workforce Intelligence, 24–25
training as sustained cadence for, 124–125
types of AI in, 119–124, 200

I

Identity threat, AI as, 138, 141–142
Impact Studio (OneDigital), 118
Individuals. *See also* Employees
AI job descriptions built around how to help, 77
personal WI playbook for, 183–186
value of, 138–143
Inputs, in Work Centers, 187
Institutional knowledge/intelligence:
growing, 69
held by human employees, 169
lack of building, 62
Integration, of AI and human intelligence, 111
Intelligence:
building maps of, 156–161
and capability, 188–189
deciding what your organization requires, 15
of hybrid workforce, 127
mapping, 25, 76, 201–202
ownership of, 68, 151–163
uniquely human, 29–30
visibility and observability of, 156–157
Internship phase, 93–96
Intrinsic motivation, for training AI, 86
Investments, in AI, 39–40
Irreducibility, 170–171
Irreducibility Test, 190–193
Iteration:
continual, for AI Coworkers, 89
in Internship phase, 95
necessary for effective AI use, 55–57
IT projects, AI transformation as, 63–65

J

J-Curve, 39–40
Jesuthasan, Ravin, 25, 76
Job descriptions, for AI Coworkers, 73–89
creating, 76–82
evolving, in three-phase lifecycle, 97
for specialist coworkers, 86–89
template for, 195–196
writing, 82–86

K

Kaplan, Robert, 36
Karry, Meagan, 19, 27, 139–142
Knowledge domain:
for AI Coworkers, 78
iterating, in Internship phase, 95
in job descriptions, 82–83, 195
Knowledge work, 144

L

Lagging firms, 40
Large language models (LLMs), 135–136
Leaders and leadership:
activating, in AI transformation, 51–55
discussing WI scores with, 181
Founder Mode posture for, 110
hiring requirements for, 56
intelligence mapping by, 159–160
lagging, in AI transformation, 13–14
modeling use of AI by, 113–114
responsibility of, to employees, 173

Leading firms, 41
Leong, Brenda, 134
Lewis, Michael, 23
LinkedIn, 63
LLMs (large language models), 135–136

M
McLean, Shelley, 75–79, 85, 95, 100–103, 115
Manager (Tier Two training), 113–114, 199
Metrics:
for behavioral shifts, 34–39
for productivity, 37
for Workforce Intelligence, 26–30. *See also* Workforce Intelligence scores
Microsoft, 34–35, 46, 63–65
Model providers, 154–155
Moderna, 65
Mollick, Ethan, 9
Monday morning checklist, 203–204
Moneyball (Lewis), 23–24

N
National Growth Strategists, 75
Nonfinancial leading indicators, 36
Norton, David, 36
Note-taking tools, 157

O
Oakland A's, 23–24
Observability, of AI Coworkers, 155–156
OneDigital, xi–xii
AI Coworkers platform at, 66–70, 88
AI transformation at, xvi
collaborative AI use at, 50–55
demonstration of collaborative AI use, 121–124
development of Workforce Intelligence at, 19–30
Fellowship program at, 108
Impact Studio of, 118
need for AI transformation at, 3–9
OneDigital Workforce Intelligence Trends Report, 41
Ongoing education:
for AI Coworkers, 86, 125
for hybrid workforce, 124–125
for Supervisors, 101–104
Opportunity Scorecard, 196–197
Orbital data centers, 146
Outputs, in Work Centers, 188
Ownership, 151–163
building intelligence maps, 156–161
building on top of models, 154–155
compounding intelligence with, 161–163
cost of lacking, 151–154
of intelligence, 68
and observability of AI Coworkers, 155–156
in Work Centers, 188

P
Performance expectations, for AI Coworkers, 84, 196
Performance reviews, of AI Coworkers, 100
Performing firms, 41
Personal WI playbook, for employees, 183–186
Personnel Administration, 20
Perspectives, finding people with different, 174
Primary responsibilities, of AI Coworkers, 83, 195
Proceedings of the National Academy of Sciences, 134
Processing, in Work Centers, 187–188
Productivity J-Curve, 39–40
Productivity ratios, 34
Product requirements documents, 77
Psychological shift, for AI use, 47

R
Raskin, Aza, 133
Rattling cages, 50–51
Redesign (AI sorting mechanism), 79–82
Redundancy, avoiding, 61, 157
Relationships, as uniquely human, 29–30, 171
Remediation, for AI Coworkers, 98, 100–101, 125
Replit, 4
Resume, of AI Coworkers, 97
Retain (AI sorting mechanism), 80, 81
Reviews, of AI Coworkers, 100
Rock, Daniel, 39
Roesler, Eileen, 134
Ruby on Rails, 50

S

Scope boundaries, for AI Coworkers, 84, 196
Security:
  of AI systems, 153
  and building AI Coworkers, 68
  and shadow AI use, 63
Self-assessments, 184–185
Selinger, Evan, 134
Seven-Dimension Opportunity Scorecard, 196–197
Shadow AI, 63
Singhvi, Robin, 94, 95, 98, 112, 125
Skills, managing for, 25–26
Society for Human Resource Management, 111
Software, treating AI as, 11–12, 63–65
Solow, Robert, 38, 39
Specialists:
  job descriptions for, 86–89
  treating AI Coworkers as, 67–68
  value offered by, enhanced with AI, 14
Stakes, in Work Centers, 188
Succession planning, 25
Sunset, for AI Coworkers, 98–99
Supervisors:
  disengaged, 99
  named in job descriptions, 84–86, 196
  ongoing education for, 101–104
  as third tier in AI fluency training, 114–115, 199–200
Syverson, Chad, 39

T

Talent:
  and AI transformation, 33
  as human and AI, 14
  judging both human and AI, 119
  shift in, measuring, 37
Taxonomy of work, for AI Coworkers, 79
37signals, 50
Thought-partners, AI as, 34–35, 45–46
Time investment, in AI training, 161–162
Transactional AI use:
  appropriate uses for, 46
  by employees, 34–35
  examples of, 45
  shifting from, 185

U

Uncertainty, 175
Utilities, 154

V

Value-creation orientation, of intelligence mapping, 160–161
Values, of firms, 169–170
Variable A, *see* AI Amplification Factor

W

Water, consumed by data centers, 145
WI, *see* Workforce Intelligence
Work Centers, 187–194
Workflows, rethinking, 53–54
Workforce, new way to visualize, 19–20. *See also* Hybrid workforce
Workforce Intelligence (WI), 19–30
  development of, 20–26
  metrics for, 26–30
  need for new way to visualize workforce, 19–20
Workforce Intelligence scores, 33–41
  calculator for, 179–182
  four bands of, 40–41
  and the J-Curve, 39–40
  measuring behavioral shifts, 34–39
Working relationships, for AI Coworkers, 83–84, 196
Work Trend Index (2024), 63

Y

Young Presidents' Organization (YPO), 25

Z

Zapier, 55–57